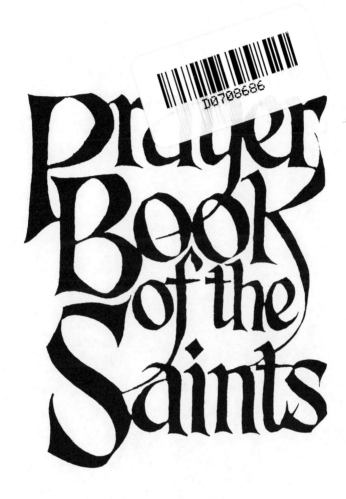

Prayer Book of the Saints

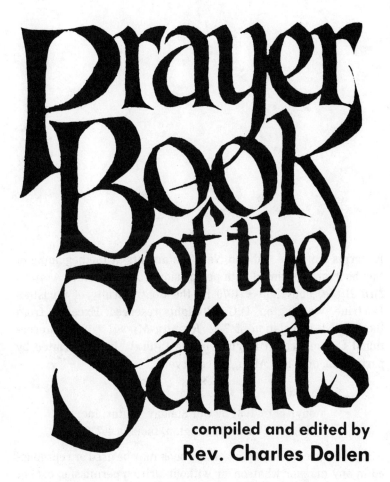

Prayer Book of the Saints

compiled and edited by
Rev. Charles Dollen

Our Sunday Visitor Inc.
200 Noll Plaza, Huntington, IN 46750

*To the kind people
of St. Gabriel's Parish, Poway, California*

Table of Contents

Preface: Saints Alive!

THE Gospels tell us consistently and persistently that Christ was a man of prayer. Over and over again He is shown withdrawing from the crowds and spending the night in prayer.

This was so obvious to His apostles and disciples that they insisted that He teach them to pray. From that insistence we have that treasure called the Lord's Prayer.

The earliest pictures of Christians show standing figures with arms outstretched in prayer. They were called *orantes* — pray-ers. Saints from as different backgrounds as St. Charles Garnier and St. Charles Lwanga were known to their converts as "the man who prays."

Modern commentators from Father Charles de Foucauld to Maisie Ward and Dorothy Day tell us that Christians must be men and women of prayer if we are to become Christ-like.

This prayer book looks at the examples of the saints across the centuries. By their lives they have shown us how to follow Christ. In their words we sing His praises.

Acknowledgements: To Mr. Bob Lockwood of Our Sunday Visitor, Inc., who suggested this work, and to the people of St. Gabriel's Parish in Poway, California, who lent me their old prayer books to collect this material. To the Confraternity of Christian Doctrine for excerpts from the *New American Bible*, and to the International Committee on English in the Liturgy, Inc., for excerpts in English from the Liturgy of the Hours (I.C.E.L.).

By Way of Prologue

THEN the LORD God said to the serpent: "Because you have done this, you shall be banned from all the animals and from all the wild creatures;

"On your belly shall you crawl, and dirt shall you eat all the days of your life.

"I will put enmity between you and the woman, and between your offspring and hers; He will strike at your head while you strike at his heel."

Genesis 3:14-15 (*Protoevangelium*)

AGAIN the LORD spoke to Ahaz: Ask for a sign from the LORD your God; let it be deep as the nether world, or high as the sky! But Ahaz answered, "I will not ask! I will not tempt the LORD!"

Then he [Isaiah] said, Listen, O house of David! Is it not enough for you to weary men, must you also weary my God? Therefore, the Lord himself will give you this sign:

The virgin shall be with child, and bear a son, and shall name him Immanuel.

Isaiah 7:10-14

I

The Church of the New Testament

DEVOUT Christians have always used the Bible as a source of their prayers. Psalms and spiritual canticles were a staple of the earliest Eucharistic Liturgies and common gatherings.

Most of us learned the Lord's Prayer and the Hail Mary at our mothers' knees. It would probably be impossible for most of us to count the number of times that we have prayed those words.

The three canticles from the Gospel of St. Luke have also been most popular in liturgical prayer: the Magnificat, the Benedictus and the Nunc Dimittis.

For the rest, it was difficult to pick and choose through the balance of Scripture, but a few of the more popular and useful are included in this section.

St. Matthew's Gospel
Chapter 6: verses 9 - 13

"**T**HIS is how you are to pray:
  'Our Father in heaven,
  hallowed be your name,
  your kingdom come,
  your will be done
  on earth as it is in heaven.
  Give us today our daily bread
  and forgive us the wrong we have done
  as we forgive those who wrong us.
  Subject us not to the trial
  but deliver us from the evil one.' "

(Taken from the *New American Bible*)

Chapter 5:3 - 12

"**H**OW blest are the poor in spirit;
  the reign of God is theirs.
Blest too are the sorrowing;
  they shall be consoled.
[Blest are the lowly;
  they shall inherit the land.]
Blest are they who hunger and thirst for holiness;
  they shall have their fill.
Blest are they who show mercy;
  mercy shall be theirs.
Blest are the single-hearted
  for they shall see God.
Blest too the peacemakers;
  they shall be called sons of God.
Blest are those persecuted for holiness' sake;

the reign of God is theirs.

Blest are you when they insult you and persecute you and
utter every kind of slander against you because of me.

Be glad and rejoice,
for your reward is great in heaven;

They persecuted the prophets before you in the very same
way.''

St. Luke's Gospel
Chapter 1:28, 42

UPON arriving, the angel [Gabriel] said to her:
"Rejoice, O highly favored daughter!
The Lord is with you,
Blessed are you among women."
Elizabeth: ". . .and blest is the fruit of your womb"
(We add). . .Jesus.
>   Holy Mary, Mother of God,
>   Pray for us sinners,
>   Now and at the hour of our death. Amen

Chapter 1: 46 - 55

THEN Mary said:
"My being proclaims the greatness of the Lord,
   my spirit finds joy in God my savior,
For he has looked upon his servant in her lowliness;
   all ages to come shall call me blessed.
God who is mighty has done great things for me,
   holy is his name;
His mercy is from age to age
   on those who fear him.
He has shown might with his arm;
   he has confused the proud in their inmost thoughts.
He has deposed the mighty from their thrones
   and raised the lowly to high places.
The hungry he has given every good thing,
   while the rich he has sent away empty.
He has upheld Israel his servant,
   ever mindful of his mercy;
Even as he promised our fathers,
   promised Abraham and his descendants forever."

Chapter 1:67 - 79

THEN Zechariah his [John's] father, filled with the
Holy Spirit, uttered this prophecy:
"Blessed be the Lord, the God of Israel
  because he has visited and ransomed his people.
He has raised up a horn of saving strength for us
  in the house of David his servant,
As he promised through the mouths of his holy ones,
  the prophets of ancient times:
Salvation from our enemies
  and from the hands of all our foes.
He has dealt mercifully with our fathers
  and remembered the holy covenant he made,
The oath he swore to Abraham our father he would grant
    us:
  that, rid of fear and delivered from the enemy,
We should serve him devoutly and through all our days
  be holy in his sight.
And you, O child, shall be called
  prophet of the Most High;
For you shall go before the Lord
  to prepare straight paths for him,
Giving his people a knowledge of salvation
  in freedom from their sins.
All this is the work of the kindness of our God;
  he, the Dayspring, shall visit us in his mercy
To shine on those who sit in darkness and in the shadow of
    death,
  to guide our feet into the way of peace."

Chapter 2: 29 - 32

Canticle of Simeon

"Now, Master, you can dismiss your servant in peace;
   you have fulfilled your word.
For my eyes have witnessed your saving deed
   displayed for all the peoples to see:
A revealing light to the Gentiles,
   the glory of your people Israel."

Chapter 10: 21 - 22

At that moment Jesus rejoiced in the Holy Spirit and said: "I offer you praise, O Father, Lord of heaven and earth, because what you have hidden from the learned and the clever you have revealed to the merest children.

"Yes, Father, you have graciously willed it so. Everything has been given over to me by my Father. No one knows the son except the Father and no one knows the Father except the Son — and anyone to whom the Son wishes to reveal him."

St. John's Gospel
Chapter 1:1 - 18

IN the beginning was the Word;
the Word was in God's presence,
and the Word was God.
He was present to God in the beginning.
Through him all things came into being,
and apart from him nothing came to be.
Whatever came to be in him found life,
life for the light of men.
The light shines on in darkness,
a darkness that did not overcome it.

There was a man named John sent by God, who came as witness to testify to the light, so that through him all men might believe — but only to testify to the light, for he himself was not the light. The real light which gives light to every man was coming into the world.

He was in the world,
and through him the world was made,
yet the world did not know who he was.
To his own he came,
yet his own did not accept him.
Any who did accept him
he empowered to become children of God.

These are they who believe in his name — who were begotten not by blood, nor by carnal desire, nor by man's willing it, but by God.

The Word became flesh
and made his dwelling among us,
and we have seen his glory:

The glory of an only Son coming from the Father,
filled with his enduring love.

John testified to him by proclaiming: "This is he of
whom I said, 'The one who comes after me ranks ahead of
me, for he was before me.' "

Of his fullness
we have all had a share
love following upon love.

For while the law was given through Moses, the enduring love came through Jesus Christ. No one has ever seen
God. It is God, the only Son, ever at the Father's side, who
has revealed him.

Chapter 6: 53 - 58

JESUS said to them:
"Let me solemnly assure you, if you do not eat the
flesh of the Son of man and drink his blood, you
have no life in you.
He who feeds on my flesh and drinks my blood has life
eternal and I will raise him up on the last day.
For my flesh is real food and my blood real drink.
The man who feeds on my flesh and drinks my blood
remains in me and I in him.
Just as the Father who has life sent me and I have life
because of the Father, so the man who feeds on me
will have life because of me.
This is the bread that came down from heaven. Unlike
your ancestors who ate and died nonetheless, the
man who feeds on this bread shall live forever."

Chapter 17: 20 - 23

I DO not pray for them [the disciples] alone. I pray also for those who will believe in me through their word, that all may be one as you, Father, are in me, and I in you.

I pray that they may be [one] in us, that the world may believe that you sent me.

I have given them the glory you gave me that they may be one as we are one — I living in them, you living in me — that their unity may be complete.

So shall the world know that you sent me and that you loved them as you loved me.

St. John's Book of Revelation
Chapter 19: excerpts (1 - 2, 5, 6 - 8, 9)

"ALLELUIA!
Salvation, glory and might belong to our God,
for his judgements are true and just!

"Praise our God all you his servants,
the small and the great who revere him!

"Alleluia!
The Lord is king, our God, the Almighty!
Let us rejoice and be glad and give him glory!
For this is the wedding day of the Lamb;
his bride has prepared herself for the wedding.
She has been given a dress to wear, made of the finest
    linen, brilliant white."
(The linen dress is the virtuous deeds of God's saints.)
    ". . .Happy are they who have been invited to the wed-
    ding feast of the Lamb."

St. Paul's Epistle to the Romans
Chapter 8:35 - 39

WHO will separate us from the love of Christ? Trial, or distress, or persecution, or hunger, or nakedness, or danger, or the sword?

As Scripture says: "For your sake we are being slain all the day long; we are looked upon as sheep to be slaughtered." Yet in all this we are more than conquerors because of him who has loved us.

For I am certain that neither death nor life, neither angels nor principalities, neither the present nor the future, nor powers, neither height nor depth nor any other creature, will be able to separate us from the love of God that comes to us in Christ Jesus, our Lord.

St. Paul's First Epistle to the Corinthians
Chapter 13:1 - 13

NOW I will show you the way which surpasses all the others.

If I speak with human tongues and angelic as well, but do not have love, I am a noisy gong, a clanging cymbal. If I have the gift of prophecy and, with full knowledge, comprehend all mysteries, if I have faith great enough to move mountains, but have not love, I am nothing. If I give everything I have to feed the poor and hand over my body to be burned, but have not love, I gain nothing.

Love is patient; love is kind. Love is not jealous, it does not put on airs, it is not snobbish. Love is never rude, it is not self-seeking, it is not prone to anger; neither does it brood over injuries. Love does not rejoice in what is wrong but rejoices with the truth. There is no limit to love's forbearance, to its trust, its hope, its power to endure.

Love never fails. Prophecies will cease, tongues will be silent, knowledge will pass away. Our knowledge is imperfect and our prophesying is imperfect. When the perfect comes, the imperfect will pass away. When I was a child I used to talk like a child, think like a child, reason like a child. When I became a man I put childish ways aside. Now we see indistinctly, as in a mirror; then we shall see face to face. My knowledge is imperfect now; then I shall know even as I am known.

There are in the end three things that remain: faith, hope and love, and the greatest of these is love.

St. Paul's Epistle to the Ephesians
Chapter 1:3 - 10

PRAISED be the God and Father of our Lord Jesus Christ, who has bestowed on us in Christ every spiritual blessing in the heavens!

God chose us in him before the world began, to be holy and blameless in his sight, to be full of love; he likewise predestined us through Christ Jesus to be his adopted sons — such was his will and pleasure — that all might praise the glorious favor he has bestowed on us in his beloved.

It is in Christ and through his blood that we have been redeemed and our sins forgiven, so immeasurably generous is God's favor to us.

God has given us the wisdom to understand fully the mystery, the plan he was pleased to decree in Christ, to be carried out in the fullness of time: namely, to bring all things in the heavens and on earth into one under Christ's headship.

St. Paul's Epistle to the Colossians
Chapter 1:12 - 20

[Give] thanks to the Father for having made you worthy to share the lot of the saints in light. He rescued us from the power of darkness and brought us into the kingdom of his beloved Son. Through him we have redemption, the forgiveness of our sins.

He is the image of the invisible God, the first-born of all creatures. In him everything in heaven and on earth was created, things visible and invisible, whether thrones or dominations, principalities or powers; all were created through him and for him.

He is before all else that is. In him everything continues in being.

It is he who is the head of the body, the church; he who is the beginning, the first-born of the dead, so that primacy may be his in everything. It pleased God to make absolute fullness reside in him and by means of him, to reconcile everything in his person, both on earth and in the heavens, making peace through the blood of his cross.

St. Peter's First Epistle
Chapter 1:3 - 15

PRAISED be the God and Father
of our Lord Jesus Christ,
he who in his great mercy
gave us new birth;
a birth unto hope which draws its life
from the resurrection of Jesus Christ from the dead;
a birth to an imperishable inheritance,
incapable of fading or defilement,
which is kept in heaven for you
who are guarded with God's power through faith;
a birth to a salvation which stands ready
to be revealed in the last days.

St. James's Epistle
Chapter 1:23 - 27

A MAN who listens to God's word but does not put it into practice is like a man who looks into a mirror at the face he was born with; he looks at himself, then goes off and promptly forgets what he looked like.

There is, on the other hand, the man who peers into freedom's ideal law and abides by it. He is no forgetful listener, but one who carries out the law in practice. Blest will this man be in whatever he does.

If a man who does not control his tongue imagines that he is devout, he is self-deceived; his worship is pointless.

Looking after orphans and widows in their distress and keeping oneself unspotted by the world make for pure worship without stain before our God and Father.

II

The Faith of Our Fathers

AFTER the fervor of the Apostolic Age, the Church went through the crucible of persecution, but the blood of the martyrs was the seed of Christians, and the Church emerged into the Age of the Fathers.

These mighty theologians had the weighty task of forming the actual wordage of Christian doctrine. Their great battles, in writings and in ecumenical councils, have had a lasting effect on how the Faith was handed down from generation to generation (Tradition) and they certainly have given color and life to our faith.

They were also men of prayer, and besides the great names such as Augustine, Basil, Ambrose and Gregory, there was a host of lesser lights whose prayers help give a special richness to this section.

The Didache or "Teaching of the Twelve Apostles" is a document so ancient that it may be contemporary to the Gospels. It contains one of the most ancient descriptions of the Eucharist. After that description, the unknown author provides a prayer of thanksgiving:

WE thank You, holy Father, for Your holy name, which You have caused to dwell in our hearts, and for the knowledge and faith and immortality which You have made known to us through Jesus Christ, Your Son; to You be glory forever.

You, Lord Almighty, have created all things for Your Name's sake, and have given food and drink and eternal life through Your Son. For all things we render You thanks, because You are mighty. To You be glory forever.

Remember, O Lord, Your Church; deliver it from all evil and make it perfect in Your love, and gather it from the four winds, sanctified for Your Kingdom which You have prepared for it, for Yours is the power and the glory forever.

Let grace come and this world pass away, "Hosanna to the God of David." If anyone is holy, let him come; if anyone is not, let him repent. Maranatha. Amen.

St. Clement of Rome was the third successor of St. Peter as Pope and Bishop of Rome (died c. 100). His letter to the Church in Corinth is a monument of early Church history. Feast: November 23.

G RANT us, O Lord, to hope in the name of Jesus, the beginning of all creation; open the eyes of our heart to know You, that You alone are the "Highest in the highest." You remain Holy among the holy.

You humble the pride of the haughty and destroy the conceits of nations, lifting up the humble and humbling the exalted. You are the helper of those in danger, the savior of those in despair, the Creator and observer of every spirit.

Through Jesus Christ Your beloved Son, You have taught us, sanctified us and given us honor. Be our helper and protector. Save those of us who are afflicted; have mercy on the humble; raise the fallen, show Yourself to those who are in need.

Let all the nations know that You alone are God, and that Jesus Christ is Your Servant, and that "we are Your people, the sheep of Your pasture."

(Chapter 59, *Letter to the Corinthians*)

St. Ignatius of Antioch was the Bishop of Antioch in Syria for forty years, after St. Peter left there (died c. 107). He wrote some famous letters that testify to the antiquity of the authentic Catholic faith. Feast: October 17.

I AM God's wheat; I am ground by the teeth of the wild beasts that I may end as the pure bread of Christ. . . .

I have no taste for the food that perishes, nor the pleasures of this life. I want the Bread of God, which is the Flesh of Christ, who was of the seed of David; and for drink I desire His Blood which is love that cannot be destroyed.

(Excerpts from his *Epistle to the Romans*)

St. Polycarp was the Bishop of Smyrna in the early second century. Feast: February 23.

LORD, God, Almighty Father of Your beloved and blessed Son Jesus Christ, through whom we have received knowledge of You, God of the angels and powers, of the whole creation and of the whole race of the righteous who live in Your sight, I bless You for having made me worthy of this day and hour.

I bless You because I may have a part, along with the martyrs, in the chalice of Your Christ, "unto resurrection in eternal life," resurrection both of soul and body in the incorruptibility of the Holy Spirit.

May I be received today as a rich and acceptable sacrifice, among those who are in Your presence, as You have prepared and foretold and fulfilled, God who is faithful and true.

For these and for all benefits I praise You, I bless You, I glorify You, through the eternal and heavenly High Priest, Jesus Christ, Your beloved Son, through whom be to You with Him and the Holy Spirit, glory, now and for all the ages to come. Amen.

(Prayer said by him at his martyrdom)

St. Irenaeus was a great apologete for the Catholic faith in the second century (130 - 202). He has a very famous and explicit history of the first line of the popes and their apostolic succession. Feast: June 28.

The Creed

THE Church, though dispersed throughout the world to the ends of the earth, has received from the Apostles and their disciples the Faith:

In one God, the Father Almighty who made the heaven and the earth and the seas, and all that is in them;

And in one Christ Jesus, the Son of God who through the prophets preached the dispensations and the advents and the birth from the Virgin, and the Passion and the resurrection from the dead and the bodily assumption into the heavens of the beloved Christ Jesus our Lord, and His appearing from the heavens in the glory of the Father, in order to sum up all things under one head and to raise up all flesh of all mankind, that to Christ Jesus our Lord and God and Savior and King, every knee of those that are in heaven and on earth and under the earth should bow according to the good pleasure of the Father, invisible, and that every tongue should confess Him and that He may execute righteous judgment on all; . . .

Sending into eternal fire the spiritual powers of wickedness and the angels who transgressed and apostatized, and the godless and unrighteous and lawless and blasphemous among men, but granting life and immortality and eternal glory to the righteous and holy who have both kept the commandments and continued in His love, some from the beginning and some from their conversion. . . .

St. Justin, Martyr, is one of the most important witnesses to the Faith and the Church from the second century (100 - 165). His description of the Mass in that century is a classic. Feast: June 1.

P OSSESSED with the desire of a life of eternal duration and purity, and striving for that abode which is above, with God the Father and Maker of all things, we hasten to confess our faith, persuaded and convinced as we are that they who have shown before God by their works that they are followers of Him, and lovers of the life that is with Him, where there is no evil to oppose, may obtain these rewards.

Our judge will be Jesus Christ, and our souls will be united to these same bodies. . . We praise Him to the best of our power with the reasonable service of prayer and thanksgiving in all our oblations.

St. Hippolytus was an important Church writer in the third century (c 180 - 236). For a short time he was an antipope, but he was reconciled to the Church before his martyrdom. Feast: August 13.

WE praise and thank You, O God, through Your Son, Jesus Christ, our Lord, through whom You have enlightened us, by revealing the light that never fades.

Night is falling and day's allotted span draws to a close. The daylight which You created for your pleasure has fully satisified us; and yet, of Your own free gift, now the evening lights do not fail us.

We praise You and glorify You through Your Son, Jesus Christ, Our Lord. Amen.

St. Cyprian, the Bishop of Carthage, was a contemporary of Pope St. Cornelius (c. 200 - 258). One of his most important books was an explanation of the Lord's Prayer. Feast: September 16.

NOT by word alone, but also by deeds has God taught us to pray, himself praying frequently and entreating and demonstrating what we ought to do by His own example.

It is written, "He retired into the desert to pray," and again, "He went up the mountain to pray, and continued to pray to God all night" (cf Luke 5:16; 6:12).

But if He who was without sin prayed, how much more ought sinners to pray? And if He watched and prayed continually, sometimes throughout the whole night, how much more ought we to lie awake at night in continual prayer!

(Edited from chapter 29, *The Lord's Prayer*)

St. Gregory Thaumaturgus (the Wonder Worker) was a bishop in the Near East (c. 200 - 268). He and his brother were converted by the theologian Origen. Feast: November 17.

MARY, you are the vessel and tabernacle containing all mysteries. You know what the patriarchs never knew; you have experienced what was never revealed to the angels; you have heard what the prophets never heard.

In a word, all that was hidden from preceding generations was made known to you; even more, most of these wonders depended on you. Amen.

St. Athanasius, the archbishop of Alexandria, fought against the Arian heresy (c. 297-373). Cardinal Newman, by studying the works of Athanasius, was led into the Catholic Church. Feast: May 2.

IT is becoming to you to be mindful of us as you stand near Him who granted you all graces, for you are the Mother of God, Queen, Lady and Mistress. Do so for the King, the Lord God and Master who was born of you.

For this reason you are called "full of grace." Remember us, most holy Virgin, and bestow on us gifts from the riches of your graces, O Virgin full of grace. Amen.

WE acknowledge the Trinity, holy and perfect, to consist of the Father, the Son, and the Holy Spirit.

In this Trinity there is no intrusion of any alien element or of anything from outside, nor is the Trinity a blend of creative and created being.

It is a wholly creative and energizing reality, self-consistent and undivided in its active power, for the Father makes all things through the Word and in the Holy Spirit, and in this way the unity of the Holy Trinity is preserved.

Accordingly in the Church one God is preached, one God "who is above all things and through all things and in all things." God is above all things as Father, for He is principle and source; He is through all things through the Word; and He is in all things in the Holy Spirit.

St. Ephraem the Deacon was born in what is present-day Syria (306 - 373). He actively opposed the heresies of his time. He has been called the Deacon of Edessa and the Harp of the Holy Spirit. Feast: June 9.

O VIRGIN most pure, wholly unspotted, O Mary, Mother of God, Queen of the universe, you are above all saints, the hope of the elect and the joy of all the blessed. It is you who have reconciled us with God, you are the only refuge of sinners and the safe harbor of those who are shipwrecked; you are the consolation of the world, the ransom of captives, the health of the weak, the joy of the afflicted and the salvation of all. We have recourse to you and we beg you to have pity on us. Amen.

O VIRGIN Immaculate, Mother of God and my Mother, from your sublime heights turn your eyes of pity upon me. Filled with confidence in your goodness and knowing full well your power, I beg you to extend to me your assistance in the journey of life, which is so full of dangers for my soul.

In order that I may never be a slave of the devil through sin but may ever live with my heart humble and pure, I entrust myself wholly to you. I consecrate my heart to you forever, my only desire being to love your divine Son, Jesus. Mary, none of your devout servants has ever perished; may I, too, be saved. Amen.

GOD of God, true God of true God, we know that You are goodness itself. Assist us in Your benevolence. Protect us lest we some day share with Satan the pains of hell. Spread over us the wings of Your mercy.

We acknowledge You as the light; we are but servants

in Your hands. Permit not that the evil one wrest us from You forever and that we rebel against Your sovereignty.

We know that You are just; be for us justice, O Lord. We know that You are our Savior; deliver and preserve us from evil. We proclaim Your holiness; sanctify us with Your Body and Blood. May the elect, who have eaten Your Flesh and drunk Your precious Blood, sing Your glory.

Grant us pardon, O God of goodness, You who are merciful to sinners. Amen.

LORD Jesus Christ, king of kings, You have power over life and death. You know what is secret and hidden, and neither our thought nor our feelings are concealed from You. Cure me of duplicity; I have done evil before You.

Now my life declines from day to day and my sins increase. O Lord, God of souls and bodies, You know the extreme frailty of my soul and my flesh. Grant me strength in my weakness, O Lord, and sustain me in my misery.

Give me a grateful soul that I may never cease to recall Your benefits, O Lord most bountiful. Be not mindful of my many sins, but forgive me all my misdeeds.

O Lord, disdain not my prayer — the prayer of a wretched sinner; sustain me with Your grace until the end, that it may protect me as in the past. It is Your grace which has taught me wisdom; blessed are they who follow her ways, for they shall receive the crown of glory.

In spite of my unworthiness, I praise You and I glorify You, O Lord, for Your mercy to me is without limit. You have been my help and my protection. May the name of Your majesty be praised forever. To You, our God, be glory. Amen.

St. Hilary of Poitiers (c. 315 - 368) was a major propo-
nent of the Catholic faith against the Arians. One of his
most famous books is on the Holy Trinity. Feast: January
13.

I AM well aware, Almighty God and Father, that in
my life I owe You a most particular duty. It is to make my
every thought and word speak to You.

Yes, in our poverty we will pray for our needs. Yours it
is, O Lord, to grant our petitions, to be present when we
seek You and to open when we knock.

We trust in You to inspire the beginnings of our work,
to strengthen its progress and to call us into a partnership
with the prophets and the apostles.

Impart to us the meaning of the words of Scripture and
the light to understand it, with reverence for the doctrine
and confidence in its truth. Grant that we may express
what we believe.

Through the prophets and the apostles we know about
You, the one God the Father and the one Lord Jesus
Christ. May we have the grace to honor You as God.
Amen.

St. Cyril of Jerusalem was a vigorous opponent of the Arian heresy (c. 315 - 387). His *Catechesis* is an explanation of the faith for catechumens. Feast: March 18.

The Creed

WE believe in one God, the Father Almighty, maker of heaven and earth and of all things, visible and invisible.

And in one Lord Jesus Christ, the Son of God, the only-begotten of the Father, true God, before all the ages, through whom all things were made:

Incarnate and made man, crucified and buried;

He rose again the third day;

And ascended into heaven;

And sat at the right hand of the Father;

And shall come again in glory to judge the quick and the dead, of whose kingdom there shall be no end.

And in one Holy Spirit, the Paraclete, who spoke through the prophets;

And in one baptism of repentance for remission of sins;

And in one, holy, Catholic Church;

And in the resurrection of the flesh;

And in the life eternal. Amen.

St. Basil the Great (c. 329-379) was the Bishop of Caesarea. He is considered the Father of Monasticism in the Eastern Churches. Feast: January 2.

WE give You thanks, O Lord our God, for the Communion of Your holy, pure and heavenly Mysteries, which You have given for the good, the hallowing and the healing of souls and bodies.

Do You, O Sovereign of the world, cause this Communion in the Holy Body and Blood of Your Christ to nourish in us unashamed faith, sincere charity, ripe wisdom, health of soul and body, separation from all ills, observance of Your Law and justification before His awful judgment seat.

O Christ our God, the mystery of Your Providence has been accomplished according to our ability. We have been reminded of Your death and we have seen a figure of Your Resurrection; we have been filled with Your infinite Life and we have tasted Your inexhaustible joy; we pray You to make us worthy of these things in the life to come through the grace of Your eternal Father and of Your holy, good, and life-giving Spirit, now and forever, eternally. Amen.

O LORD our God, teach us, we beseech You, to ask for the gift we need. Steer the ship of our life to Yourself, the quiet harbor of all storm-stressed souls.

Show us the course which we are to take. Renew in us the spirit of docility. Let Your Spirit curb our fickleness; guide and strengthen us to perform what is for our own good, to keep Your commandments and ever to rejoice in Your glorious and vivifying presence. Yours is the glory and praise for all eternity. Amen.

St. Gregory Nazianzen (c. 330 - 390) was an Archbishop of Constantinople who vigorously fought against heresy. So greatly respected were his talents that he is called simply "the Theologian." Feast: September 13.

O CHRIST Our Lord, strengthen the foundations of Your Church. Let singleness of heart take deep root in us. Guide us in the way of holiness.

Bestow on the clergy grace; to monks, give endurance; to virgins, purity; give a good life to those who are married; to those who are in penitence, give mercy; goodness to the rich; meekness to the humble; give aid to the poor; strengthen the aged, teach the converts, convert unbelievers; let divisions in the Church be healed. Destroy the pride of heretics. Reckon us all among the pious.

Remember, O Lord, my poverty: forgive me my sins. In the place where iniquity abounds, let Your grace abound. Take not away from Your people the grace of the Holy Spirit.

Have mercy on us, O God our Savior; have mercy on us, O God our Savior; have mercy on us, O God our Savior: give to Your people singleness of heart! Amen.

LORD and Creator of all, especially of Your creature man, You are the God and Father and ruler of all Your children; You are the Lord of life and death, the guardian and benefactor of our souls.

You fashion and transform all things in their due course through Your creative Word, as You know to be the best in Your great wisdom and Providence. Receive those who have gone ahead of us in our journey from this life.

Receive us, too, at the proper time when You have guided us in our earthly life as long as You see it is good. May we set out eagerly for that everlasting and blessed life which is in Jesus Christ, Our Lord. To Him be glory for ever and ever. Amen.

LORD Jesus, You want us to become a living force for all mankind, lights shining in the world. You want us to become radiant lights as we stand beside You, the great light, bathed in Your glory, O Light of Heaven.

Let us enjoy more and more the pure and dazzling light of the Holy Trinity, as now we have received, though not in its fullness, a ray of its splendor, proceeding from the one true God, in Christ Jesus our Lord, to whom be glory and power for ever and ever. Amen.

St. Ambrose, born in Germany, was the Bishop of Milan (c. 340 - 397). He was one of the strongest opponents of Arianism, a particularly pernicious heresy of the fourth century. Feast: December 7.

COME Holy Spirit, who ever one
Are with the Father and the Son,
It is the hour; our souls possess
With Your full flood of holiness.

Let flesh and heart and lips and mind
Sound fourth our witness to mankind;
And love light up our mortal frame,
Till others catch the living flame.

Grant this, O Father, ever one,
With Christ, Your sole-begotten Son,
And Holy Spirit, whom all adore,
Reigning and blest forevermore.

LORD, Jesus Christ, You are so kind, no merits of my own invite me to the pleasures of Your banquet table. I am a sinner and I come in fear and trembling, encouraged only by Your mercy and goodness.

My soul and body are defiled with many sinful deeds. My tongue and heart have run their course without restraint, God of gracious kindness, while I tremble before Your majesty; wretch that I am, trapped in my own insufficiency, I still look to You, the source of mercy. I hasten to You to be healed and to seek refuge under Your protection. I yearn to have You for my Savior for I cannot stand before You as my judge.

Lord, I show You my wounds and uncover my shame before You. My many great sins are known to me and they make me afraid. But I hope in Your mercy which knows no limits. Turn Your merciful gaze toward me, Lord Jesus Christ, eternal King, God and man, crucified for mankind. Hear my cry of hope. Pity one so full of sin and wretchedness, for You are the inexhaustible fountain of forgiveness.

Hail, Victim who saves, offered for me and for all men on the gallows of the Cross. Hail, noble Blood beyond price, flowing from the wounds of my crucified Lord Jesus Christ and washing away the sins of the world. Remember, Lord, Your creation which You have redeemed with Your Precious Blood.

I am sorry that I have sinned and I want to make up for what I have done. Take all sin and evil away from me, Father of mercy, so that, clean in body and soul, I may be fit to appreciate this holy of holies.

Grant also that this offering of Your Body and Blood, which in my unworthiness I am to receive, may forgive my sins, cleanse me utterly of my crimes and dispel sinful thoughts.

May it then revive my holy desires, give me the saving strength to do what You desire, and protect me securely against the traps of my enemies. Amen.

O LORD, You are all merciful; take away my sins from me, and enkindle within me the fire of Your Holy Spirit. Take away this heart of stone and give me a heart of flesh and blood, a heart to love and adore You, a heart which may delight in You, love You and please You, for Jesus' sake. Amen.

Pope St. Damasus (d. 384) is most famous because he commissioned St. Jerome to translate the Bible into the common (or vulgar) Latin. During his long pontificate he developed the Roman liturgy. Feast: December 11.

(O GREAT St. Andrew), your name, a token of beauty, foretells your splendor in the glory of your holy cross.

The cross exalts you, the blessed cross loves you, the bitter cross prepares the joys of the light to come for you.

The mystery of the cross shines in you with a twofold beauty: for by the cross you vanquished insults and taught all mankind of the Divine Blood shed on the cross.

Give fervor to our languid hearts and take us under your care that by the victory of the cross we may reach our home in heaven. Amen.

St. Jerome is probably the greatest Scripture scholar ever known in the Christian Church (c. 343 - 420). He is called "the Father of Biblical Science." Feast: September 30.

SHOW me, O Lord, Your mercy and delight my heart with it. Let me find You, since I seek You with such great longing.

Behold, here is the man whom the robbers seized, mishandled and left half dead on the road to Jericho. O kind-hearted Samaritan! Come to my aid.

I am the sheep who wandered into the wilderness; seek after me and bring me back to Your fold. Do with me according to Your will that I may abide with You all the days of my life and praise You with all those who are now with You in heaven, for all eternity. Amen.

St. John Chrysostom was the Archbishop of Constantinople at the turn of the fifth century (c. 347 - 407). He is famous for his homilies and scriptural commentaries. He is considered the greatest of the Greek Fathers. Feast: September 13.

O LORD and lover of men, shine in our hearts the pure light of Your divine knowledge, and open the eyes of our mind to the understanding of Your Gospel teaching.

Instill in us the fear of Your blessed commandments, that, trampling upon all carnal desires, we may enter on a spiritual life, willing and doing all that is Your good pleasure.

For You are the light of our souls and of our bodies, Christ O God, and we give glory to You, together with Your eternal Father and Your all-holy, good, and life-giving Spirit, now and forever, world without end. Amen.

(Liturgy)

St. Augustine was the Bishop of Hippo in North Africa (354-430). He is famous for such books as the *Confessions, The City of God* and *On the Holy Trinity.* He is called the Doctor of Grace. Feast: August 28.

O LORD our God, we believe in You, Father, Son and Holy Spirit. As far as I have been able, as much as You have given me the power to do so, I have sought after You. I have desired to see that in which I believe; much have I worked for this.

Lord, my God, my only hope, let me never tire of seeking You, but make me seek Your face with constant ardor. Give me the strength for this task.

You see my strength and my weakness; sustain the one and heal the other. You see my strength and my ignorance. Where You have closed things to me, open to my plea; what You have opened to me, make me welcome.

Give me to remember, understand and trust You.

St. Augustine: *Confessions,* Book 10, chapter 27.

LATE have I loved You, O Beauty ever ancient, ever new; late have I loved You! Behold, You were within and I was without. I was looking for You out there and I threw myself, deformed as I was, upon those well-formed things which You had made. You were with me, yet I was not with You. These "things" held me so far from you, things which would not have existed had they not been in You. You called and cried out and burst in on my deafness; You shined forth and glowed and drove away my blindness; You sent forth Your fragrance and I drew in my breath, and now I pant for You. I have tasted and now I hunger and thirst. You touched me and I was inflamed with desire for Your peace.

• • • •

We are Easter people and alleluia is our song!

LORD Jesus, let me know myself and know You,
And desire nothing save only You.
Let me deny myself and love You.
Let me do everything for Your sake.
Let me humble myself and exalt You.
Let me think of nothing except of You.
Let me die to myself and live in You.
Let me accept whatever happens as from You.
Let me banish self and follow You,
And ever desire to follow You.
Let me fly from myself and take refuge in You,
That I may deserve to be defended by You.
Let me fear for myself, let me fear You,
And let me be among those who are chosen by You.
Let me distrust myself and put my trust in You.
Let me be willing to obey for your sake.
Let me cling to nothing save only You,
And let me be poor because of You.
Look upon me that I may love You,
And forever enjoy You. Amen.

O BLESSED Virgin Mary, who can worthily give you the just dues of praise and thanksgiving, you who by the wondrous assent of your will rescued a fallen world? What songs of praise can our weak human nature recite in your honor, since it is by your intervention alone that it has found the way to restoration?

Accept, then, such poor thanks as we have to offer here, though they be unequal to your merit; and, receiving our vows, obtain by your prayers the remission of our offenses. Carry our prayers within the sanctuary of the heavenly audience and bring forth the gift of our reconciliation.

Take our offering, grant us our requests, obtain pardon for what we fear, for you are the sole hope of sinners. Holy Mary, help the miserable, strengthen the fainthearted, comfort the sorrowful, pray for your people, plead for the clergy, intercede for all women consecrated to God.

Be ever ready to assist us when we pray and bring back to us the answers to our prayers. Make it your continual care to pray for the people of God, you who, blessed by God, merited to bear the Redeemer of the world who lives and reigns, world without end. Amen.

St. Cyril of Alexandria was the Archbishop of Alexandria in Egypt (c. 376 - 444). He presided at the Council of Ephesus and wrote many learned theological treatises. Feast: June 27.

HAIL, Mother and Virgin, imperishable temple of the Godhead, venerable treasure of the whole world, crown of virginity, support of the true faith on which the Church is founded throughout the whole world.

Mother of God, who contained the infinite God under your heart, whom no space can contain: Through you the Most Holy Trinity is adored and glorified, demons are vanquished, Satan cast down from heaven into hell and our fallen nature again assumed into heaven.

Through you the human race, held captive in the bonds of idolatry, arrives at the knowledge of the truth. What more shall I say of you? Hail, through whom kings rule, through whom the only-begotten Son of God has become a star of light to those who were sitting in darkness and in the shadow of death. Amen.

St. Macarius was one of two Egyptian "Desert Fathers" of the same name (fourth century). To these men the famous JESUS PRAYER is ascribed. Feast: January 15.

The prayer is a living call of faith in the Name of Our Lord. It may be a simple, and repeated, use of the Name of Jesus, or it may be the repetition of a slightly longer form:

> LORD Jesus Christ,
> Son of the Living God,
> Have mercy on me, a sinner.

St. Nicetas was the Bishop of Remesiana in what is now Serbia (335 - 415). He is most famous for this prayer-hymn, the *Te Deum,* which is still used regularly in the Divine Office. Feast: June 22.

YOU are God — we praise You;
You are the Lord — we acclaim You;
You are the eternal Father:
All creation worships You.
To You all the angels of Heaven and all the powers,
Cherubim and Seraphim, sing in endless praise —
   Holy, holy, holy, Lord, God of power and might,
   heaven and earth are full of Your glory.
The glorious company of apostles praise you;
The noble fellowship of the prophets praise You;
The white-robed army of martyrs praise You,
Throughout the world Holy Church acclaims you:
   Father of majesty unbounded,
   Your true and only Son, worthy of all worship,
   And the Holy Spirit, advocate and guide.
You, O Christ, are the king of glory,
The eternal Son of the Father.
When You became man to set us free, You did not spurn
   the virgin's womb.
You overcame the sting of death and opened the kingdom
   of heaven to all believers.
You are seated at God's right hand in robes of glory.
We believe that You will come to be our Judge.
Come then, Lord, and help Your people bought with the
   price of Your own Precious Blood, and bring us with
   Your saints to glory everlasting.

St. Patrick is the famous missionary of Ireland (389 - 461). He worked for almost thirty years to establish a lasting Church there. Feast: March 17.

Breastplate of St. Patrick

CHRIST be with me, Christ before me,
   Christ be after me, Christ within me,
Christ beneath me, Christ above me,
Christ at my right hand, Christ at my left,
Christ in the fort, Christ in the chariot,
Christ in the ship,
Christ in the heart of every man who thinks of me,
Christ in the mouth of every man who speaks of me,
Christ in every ear that hears me.

MAY the strength of God pilot us.
May the power of God preserve us.
May the wisdom of God instruct us.
May the hand of God protect us.
May the way of God direct us.
May the shield of God defend us.
May the host of God guard us against the snares
   of the Evil One and the temptations of the world.

AT Tara today, in this awful hour
   I call in the Holy Trinity:
Glory to Him who reigns in power,
The God of the elements, Father and Son
And Paraclete Spirit, which Three are the One,
   The ever-existing Divinity!

At Tara today I call on the Lord,

On Christ, the omnipotent Word,
Who came to redeem us from death and sin,
  Our fallen race.
  And I put and I place
The virtue that lies and lives in
  His Incarnation lowly,
  His Baptism pure and holy,
His life of toil and tears and affliction,
His dolorous Death, His Crucifixion,
His Burial, sacred and sad and lone,
  His Resurrection to life again,
His glorious Ascension to heaven's high throne,
And, lastly, His future dread
  And terrible coming to judge all men,
Both the living and the dead. . . .

St. Benedict of Nursia was the founder of the Benedictines, and indeed, the Father of Western Monasticism (408 - 547). He was declared the Patron of Europe by Pope Paul VI. Feast: July 11.

O LORD, I place myself in Your hands and dedicate myself to You. I pledge myself to do Your will in all things — to love the Lord God with all my heart, all my soul, all my strength.

Not to kill or steal; not to covet or bear false witness. To honor all persons. Not to do to another what I would not wish done to myself. To chastise the body and not to seek after pleasures.

To love fasting and to relieve the poor; to clothe the naked and to visit the sick; to bury the dead and to help those in trouble. To console the sorrowing and to hold myself aloof from wordly ways. To prefer nothing to the love of Christ.

Not to give way to anger nor to foster a desire for revenge; not to entertain deceit in the heart nor to make a false peace; not to forsake charity nor to swear, lest I swear falsely.

To speak the truth with heart and tongue and not to return evil for evil; to do no evil and, indeed, even to bear patiently any injury done to me. To love my enemies and not to curse those who curse me — but rather to bless them.

To bear persecution for justice's sake and not to be proud. Not to delight in intoxicating drink, nor to be an overeater; not to be lazy or slothful; not to be a murmurer or a detractor.

To put my trust in God and to refer the good I see in myself to God; to refer any evil in myself to myself, and to fear the day of judgment. To be in dread of hell and to desire eternal life with ardent longing; to keep death before my eyes daily and to keep constant watch over my words and deeds.

To remember that God sees me everywhere and so to call upon Christ for defense against evil thoughts that spring up in my heart. To guard my tongue against wicked speech and, indeed, to avoid much speaking. To avoid idle talk and not try to be considered clever.

To read only what is good to read and to look at only what is good to see. To pray often. To ask forgiveness daily for my sins and to look for ways to amend my life. To obey my superiors in all legitimate things, not to be thought holy so much as to be holy.

To fulfill the commandments of God through good works. To love chastity and to hate no one. Not to be jealous or envious of anyone, nor to love strife and pride. To honor the aged and to pray for my enemies. To make peace after a quarrel before sunset and never to despair of Your mercy, O God of Mercy. Amen.

Pope St. Gregory the Great was the first of many popes to have the name (540 - 604). He vigorously opposed the heresies of his time and wrote many learned theological works. Feast: September 3.

LOOK down, O Sovereign Creator of the world, our Ruler, and cast out from us all sinful sloth. We implore You, all-holy Christ, to forgive our sins. Help us as we rise during the night to chant Your praises.

By night we lift up our hands and hearts as the prophet commands us to do. St. Paul also gave us the example by his words and actions.

You see the evil we have done; we lay bare our secret faults; sighing, we pour forth our prayers; pardon whatever we have done amiss.

Grant this, O Father, only Son and Spirit, God of grace, to whom all worship shall be offered in every time and place. Amen.

HEAR our prayers, O loving Creator, poured forth with our tears during this sacred forty-day fast.

Loving searcher of hearts, You know our weakness, You know our strength; grant the grace of pardon to those of us who have turned back to You.

Much indeed have we sinned, but spare us as we confess our misdeeds; for the glory of Your name, grant a remedy to the weak.

Grant that through abstinence our bodies may be brought into subjection, so that our hearts, being free from sin, may abandon the food of sin.

Grant, O Blessed Trinity and simple Unity, that the rewards of fasting may be profitable to Your servants. Amen.

St. Columban was an Irish monk and scholar (545 - 615). He founded several famous monasteries in Western Europe. Feast: November 23.

MERCIFUL God, good Lord, I wish You would unite me to that fountain from which I might drink of the living spring of the water of life with those others who thirst after You.

There in that heavenly region may I ever dwell, delighted with abundant goodness, and say, "How sweet is the fountain of living water which never fails, the water welling up into eternal life."

O God, You Yourself are that fountain, ever to be desired, ever to be consumed. Lord Christ, always give us this water to be for us the source of life. I ask You for Your great benefits.

You are our all: our life and our light, our food and our drink, our salvation and our God.

St. Venantius Fortunatus was the Bishop of Poitiers, in France (530 - 609). While he is not listed in the Roman Martyrology, his feast is celebrated in several dioceses in France and Germany. Feast: December 14.

THE God whom earth and sea and sky
Adore and laud and magnify,
Whose might they own, whose praise they tell,
In Mary's body deigned to dwell.

O Mother blest! the chosen shrine
Wherein the Architect divine,
Whose hand contains the earth and sky,
Vouchsafed in hidden guise to lie:

Blest in the message Gabriel brought;
Blest in the work the Spirit wrought;
Most blest, to bring to human birth
The long-desired of all the earth.

O Lord the Virgin bore, to Thee
Eternal praise and glory be,
Whom with the Father we adore
And Holy Spirit for ever more.

SING, my tongue, the glorious battle
    Sing the last, the dread affray;
O'er the Cross, the victor's trophy,
    Sound the high triumphal lay;
Tell how Christ, the world's Redeemer,
    As a victim won the day.

God, His Maker, sorely grieving,
    That the first-made Adam fell,

When he ate the fruit of sorrow,
  Whose reward was death and hell,
Noted then this Wood, the ruin
  Of the ancient wood to quell.

For the work of our salvation
  Needs would have his order so,
And the multiform deceiver's
  Art by art would overflow,
And from thence would bring the medicine,
  Whence the insult of the foe.

Wherefore, when the sacred fullness
  Of the appointed time has come,
This world's Maker left His Father,
  Sent the heavenly mansion from,
And proceeded, God Incarnate
  Of the Virgin's holy womb.

Weeps the Infant in the manger
  That in Bethlehem's stable stands;
And His limbs the Virgin Mother
  Did compose in swaddling bands,
Meetly thus in linen folding
  Of her God the feet and hands.

Thirty years among us dwelling,
  His appointed time fulfilled,
Born for this, He meets His Passion,
  For that this He freely willed;
On the Cross the Lamb is lifted,
  Where His life-blood shall be spilled.

He endured the nails, the spitting,
  Vinegar, and spear, and reed;
From that holy Body broken,

Blood and water forth proceed:
Earth and stars and sky and ocean
   By that flood from stain are freed.

Faithful Cross! above all other
   One and only noble Tree!
None in foliage, none in blossom,
   None in fruit thy peers may be
Sweetest wood and sweetest iron,
   Sweetest weight is hung on thee.

Bend your boughs, O Tree of glory,
   Your relaxing sinews bend;
For a while the ancient rigor
   That your birth bestowed, suspend;
And the King of heavenly beauty
   On your bosom gently tend.

You alone were counted worthy
   This world's ransom to uphold:
For a shipwrecked race preparing
   Harbor, like the Ark of old;
With the sacred Blood anointed
   From the smitten lamb that rolled.

To the Trinity be glory
   Everlasting, as is meet;
Equal to the Father, equal
   To the Son, and Paraclete:
Trinal Unity, whose praises
   All created things repeat.

THE banners of the King come forth; brightly beams the mystery of the Cross on which Life suffered death and, by His death, obtained life for us.

He was wounded by the cruel point of a spear and there issued forth blood and water to cleanse us from the defilements of sin.

Now is fulfilled what David foretold in psalms, saying to the nations, "God has reigned from a tree."

O Beautiful and resplendent Tree adorned with the purple of the King, chosen to bear on your worthy trunk, limbs so holy.

O blessed Tree upon whose branches hung the ransom of the world; the beam which supported that Body snatched away hell's expected prey.

Hail, O Cross, our hope. In this passiontide increase grace in the just and, for sinners, blot out their sins.

May every spirit praise the Holy Trinity, the fount of salvation; those to whom You gave the victory of the Cross, grant also the reward.

St. Germanus was the Patriarch of Constantinople (c. 660 - 732). He vigorously defended the Catholic faith in the face of the heresies of the eighth century. Feast: May 12.

WHO could know God, were it not for you, most holy Mary? Who could be saved? Who would be preserved from dangers? Who would receive any grace, were it not for you, Mother of God, full of grace? What hope could we have of salvation, if you abandon us, O Mary, who are the life of Christians?

St. Bede the Venerable is the only English saint listed among the Fathers of the Church (c. 673 - 735). He is also called the Father of English history. This is his deathbed prayer. Feast: May 25.

IF it so please my Maker, it is time for me to return to Him who created me and formed me out of nothing when I did not exist. I have lived a long time, and the righteous Judge has taken good care of me during my whole life.

The time has come for my departure, and I long to die and be with Christ. My soul yearns to see Christ, my King, in all His glory.

Glory be to the Father, and to the Son and to the Holy Spirit.

St. John Damascene was a Syrian monk noteworthy because of his many writings (c. 675 - 749). He was called "the Golden Speaker" because of his eloquence. Feast: December 4.

I STAND before the gates of Your temple, O Lord, and yet my grievous thoughts do not leave me. You, O Christ my God, justified the publican, had mercy on the Canaanite woman, and opened the gates of Paradise to the thief on the cross; open to me the fount of Your compassionate mercy and receive me as I come to You and touch You, even as the sinful woman and the sick woman; for one touched but the hem of Your garment and was healed; the other, embracing Your feet, received full forgiveness of her sins.

But I, miserable sinner, dare to partake of Your Precious Blood; let me not be consumed. Receive me as You did them. Enlighten my spirit and sense; destroy my sinful errors, through the prayers of Your holy Mother and of all the heavenly hosts. Blessed are You to ages and ages. Amen.

HAIL Mary, hope of Christians, hear the prayers of a sinner who loves you tenderly, who honors you in a special manner, who places in you the hope of his salvation. I owe you my life.

Obtain for me the grace of your divine Son, You are the sure pledge of my eternal happiness. I entreat you, deliver me from the burden of my sins, take away the darkness of my mind, destroy the earthly affections of my heart, defeat the temptations of my enemies and rule all the actions of my life so that with you as guide I may arrive at the eternal happiness of heaven. Amen.

O LORD, You have led me from my father's loins and formed me in my mother's womb. You brought me, a naked baby, into the light of day, for nature's laws always obey your commands.

By the blessings of the Holy Spirit You prepared my creation and my existence; not because man willed it or flesh desired it, but by Your ineffable grace. You sent me forth into the light by adopting me as Your son, and You enrolled me among the children of Your holy and spotless Church, through baptism.

You nursed me with the spiritual milk of Your divine words. You kept me alive with the solid food of the Body of Jesus Christ and You let me drink from the chalice of His life-giving Blood, poured out to save the whole world.

Now You have called me by the hand of Your bishop to minister to Your people. Purify my mind and heart to lead Your people in truth.

You, O Church, are a most noble assembly whose assistance comes from God. You in whom God lives, receive from us an exposition of the faith that is free from error, to strengthen the Church, just as our fathers handed it down to us. Amen.

O DAY of Resurrection! Let us be filled with festive joy. Today is the Lord's own Passover, for from death to life, from earth to heaven Christ has led us.

Let us shout the victory hymn —
  Christ is risen from the dead!

Let our hearts be spotless as we gaze upon the dazzling Christ; see His rising, a brilliant flash of divine light. Let us listen and clearly hear Him greet us —

Let us shout the victory hymn —
  Christ is risen from the dead!

Let all heaven burst forth with hymns of joy; let all the earth resound with gladness. Let all creation dance in celebration, for Christ has risen, Christ our lasting joy.

Let us shout the victory hymn —
  Christ is risen from the dead.

St. Paulinus was the Patriarch of Aquileia, in Italy (726 - 802). He was a faithful friend and helper for Charlemagne. Feast: January 28.

WHATSOEVER you shall bind on earth with chains, O Peter, shall be bound in the stronghold of the skies, and what here the power bestowed on you loosens, shall be loosed in heaven's exalted height: at the end of the world you will judge mankind.

To God the Father be glory through endless ages; eternal Son, may we sing Your glorious praises; heavenly Spirit, to You be honor and glory. Unceasingly may the Holy Trinity be praised through all eternity. Amen.

III

Our Medieval Heritage

A S the early Middle Ages began, the Roman Empire was more a thing on paper than an actual fact. In the general breakup in Western civilization, the monasteries became the great beacons to preserve the faith.

St. Bernard of Clairvaux was the first great light to emerge, and he bridges the centuries between Augustine and Thomas Aquinas. Historically, these are the three most influential theologians in the Western Church, at least up until the Counter-Reformation.

The high Middle Ages witnessed the birth of the Franciscans, the Dominicans and a host of imitators. In fact, William Thomas Walsh titled his book about this century: *Thirteenth, Greatest of Centuries.*

Internal conflict in the Church weakened the growth of the rich imagery and symbolism of the prayer life of the people as the Church hovered on the verge of the Protestant Reformation.

However, devotion to Mary through the Rosary emerged from these troubled times, and women saints began to make their writings noticed.

St. Odo of Cluny was the abbot of that celebrated Benedictine monastery (879 - 942). He promoted the religious life in France and Italy. Feast: November 18.

O ONLY-begotten Son of the sovereign Father, look upon us with a benign countenance. It is You who called the penitent heart of the Magdalene to the pinnacle of glory.

The lost penny is again restored to the royal treasury; and the gem wiped clean from mire surpasses the stars in brilliance.

O Jesus, balm on our wounds and sole hope of the penitent, through the tears of the Magdalene wash away our sins.

O most gracious Mother of God, take us, the weeping descendants of Eve, from a thousand waves in this life to a haven of safety.

To God alone be glory for His manifold graces — to God who forgives the sins of sinners and bestows rewards. Amen.

SS. Cyril and Methodius were the apostles of the Slavic peoples (ninth century). They developed the Slavonic, or Cyrillic, alphabet. Feast: February 14.

O LORD, my God, You have created the choirs of angels and spiritual powers. You have stretched forth the heavens and established the earth, creating all that exists from nothing.

You hear those who obey Your will and keep Your commandments in holy fear. Hear my prayer and protect Your faithful people. Keep them free from harm and the worldly cunning of those who blaspheme You.

Build up Your Church and gather all into unity. Make Your people known for the unity of their profession of faith. Inspire the hearts of Your people with Your word and teaching.

May all praise and glorify Your name, the Father, Son and Holy Spirit. Amen.

(Prayer of St. Cyril)

St. Peter Damian was a Benedictine and a cardinal (1007 - 1072). He worked zealously for the spiritual perfection of the Church. Feast: February 21.

Have mercy, Lord, on all my friends and relatives, on all my benefactors, on all who pray to You for me, and on all who have asked me to pray for them. Give them the spirit of fruitful penance; mortify in them all vices, and make them flower in all Your virtues.

Let them, O Lord, so live in all that they may be pleasing to Your majesty by their good conversation. Have mercy, O God, on our bishops, our rulers, our governments and on the whole Christian people.

Holy Mary, pray for them all. All you saints of God, pray for them. Have mercy, O God, on all my deceased benefactors and on all for whom I ought to pray. Absolve all Your faithful and give them peace and communion with all Your saints.

Holy Virgin Mary, pray for them all. All you saints of God, pray for them all. Amen.

Blessed Herman the Cripple was a Swiss monk (1014 - 1054). He was famous for his prayer-filled poetry. Feast September 25.

O LOVING Mother of the Redeemer
Gate of Heaven, Star of the Sea,
Assist your people who have fallen, yet strive to rise
 again.

To the wonder of nature you bore your Creator,
Yet remained a virgin, after as before.
You who received Gabriel's joyful greeting,
Have pity on us poor sinners.

St. Anselm of Canterbury was an Italian Benedictine who was named Archbishop of Canterbury in England (1033 - 1109). He is famous for his writings on the Incarnation and on atonement. He is called the Father of Scholasticism. Feast: April 21.

O MERCIFUL Almighty Father, You pour down Your benefits upon us; forgive the unthankfulness with which we have requited Your goodness.

We have remained before You with dead, unfeeling hearts, not kindled with the love of Your gentle and enduring goodness. Turn to us, O merciful Father.

Make us hunger and thirst for You with our whole hearts. With all our longings let us desire You. Make us serve You — You, alone — with all of our heart. With all our zeal help us desire only those things that are pleasing to You.

We ask this for the sake of Your only-begotten Son, to whom, with You and the Holy Spirit, be all honor and all glory, Lord, forevermore. Amen.

WE love You, O God, and desire to love You more and more. Grant that we may love You as we wish to love You and as we should love You. O dearest Friend who has loved us so deeply and redeemed us; come and take Your place in our hearts. Watch over our lips, our steps and our deeds and we need no longer fear for soul and body.

Yes, give us love, most precious of gifts, which knows no enemies. Give our hearts that pure love borne on Your love for us, that we may love others as You love us. O Most loving Father of Jesus Christ from whom all love flows, grant that our hearts, frozen in sin and grown cold toward You, may be warmed in the divine glow. Help and bless us in Your Son.

O Blessed Lord, You have commanded us to love one another; give us the grace that, as we have received Your unmerited favors, we may love all persons in You and for You. We implore Your clemency for all people, but particularly for our friends whom You have given us. Love them, Source of Love, and instill in them a thorough love of Yourself, that they may seek, utter and do nothing save what is pleasing to You. Amen.

O GOD! You are life, wisdom, truth, goodness and happiness. You are the eternal, the only true good. My Lord and my God! You are my hope and the joy of my heart. I profess it and thank You that You have fashioned me in Your own image, so that I may fix all my thoughts on You and ever love You.

Grant, O Lord, that I may truly realize that I may ever love You more and more and joyfully possess You. And, as I cannot fully win this happiness in the life here below, grant at least that it may grow in me day by day, until it is fully realized in the life to come.

Let the knowledge of You flourish here, and let it be perfected there, so that here my joy may be great in hope, and there perfected in realization. Amen.

BLESSED Lady, sky and stars, earth and rivers, day and night, everything that is subject to the power or use of man, rejoice that through you they are in some sense restored to their lost beauty and are endowed with new grace.

The world, contrary to its true destiny, was corrupted and tainted by the actions of men. Now all creation has been restored to life and rejoices that it is controlled and given splendor by those who believe in God.

Through the fullness of the grace that was given to

you, created things rejoice in their liberty, and those in heaven are glad to be made new. Through the Son, who was the glorious fruit of your womb, just souls exult and the angels rejoice at the restoration of their shattered domain.

God, then, is the Father of the created world and Mary the mother of the re-created world. God is the Father through whom all things were given life; Mary the Mother through whom all things were given new life. For God begot the Son through whom all things were made, and Mary gave birth to Him as the Savior of the world.

Without God's Son, nothing could exist; without Mary's Son, nothing could be redeemed. Truly, the Lord is with you, O Mary, to whom the Lord granted that all nature should owe so much to you.

St. Bernard of Clairvaux helped spread the Cistercian monks throughout Europe (c. 1090 - 1153), and he was a mystical theologian of profound depth. He has been called the "last of the Fathers." He is titled Doctor Mellifluous. Feast: August 20.

OH, how good and pleasant a thing it is to dwell in the Heart of Jesus! who is there that does not love a heart so wounded? Who can refuse a return of love to a heart so loving?

O JESUS, admirable king and noble conqueror, sweetness ineffable, wholly to be desired:

When You visit our heart, then truth illuminates it; the vanity of the world becomes contemptible, and charity glows within.

O Jesus, sweetness of hearts, living fountain, light of intellects, You surpass all joys and all desires.

Let all confess Jesus, let all earnestly ask for His love; let all zealously seek Jesus and in seeking Him become enkindled with love.

May our voices praise You, O Jesus; may the whole course of our lives give testimony to You; may our hearts love You now and forever. Amen.

JESUS! How sweet is the very thought of You, giving true joy to the heart; but surpassing honey and all sweetness in His own presence.

Nothing more sweet can be proclaimed, nothing more pleasant can be heard, nothing more loving can be thought of than Jesus, the Son of God.

O Jesus, the hope of penitents, how kind You are to

those who pray. How good to those who seek You — but what to those who find!

No tongue can tell, nor can the written word express it: only one who knows from experience can say what it means to love Jesus.

May You, O Jesus, be our joy as You will be our reward. In You be our glory forever.

POWERFUL, sovereign Queen, come to our aid. Speak for us to Our Lord Jesus Christ, Who can do it better than you, who conversed so intimately with Him here on earth, and now so fully possess Him in heaven?

Speak to your Son for us. He cannot refuse you anything. Ask for us a great love of God, perseverance in His holy grace, and the happiness of dying in His friendship, that we may see you and thank you with Him eternally. Amen.

The Memorare

REMEMBER, O most gracious Virgin Mary, that never was it known that anyone who fled to your protection, implored your aid or sought your intercession, was left unaided.

Inspired with this confidence I fly unto you, O Virgin of virgins, my Mother; to you do I come, before you I stand, sinful and sorrowful; O Mother of the Word Incarnate, despise not my petitions, but in your mercy, hear and answer me. Amen.

St. Francis of Assisi founded the Franciscan Order (1182 - 1226). He is certainly the most ecumenical of all the saints in the Roman martyrology. He is the patron saint of ecologists. Feast: October 4.

I BELIEVE that You are present in the Blessed Sacrament, O Jesus. I love You and desire You. Come into my heart.

I embrace You; O never leave me. I beg You, O Lord Jesus, that the burning and most sweet power of Your love absorb my mind, that I may die through love of Your love, since You graciously died for love of my love.

Prayer of St. Francis

MAKE me, O Lord, an instrument of Your peace.

Where there is hatred, let me sow love;
Where there is injury, pardon;
Where there is doubt, faith;
Where there is despair, hope;
Where there is darkness, light;
Where there is sadness, joy.

O Divine Master, grant that I may not so much seek to be consoled as to console; to be understood as to understand; to be loved as to love;

For it is in giving that we receive; it is in pardoning that we are pardoned, and it is in dying that we are born to eternal life. Amen.

(Apparently composed under his influence)

Canticle of Brother Sun

O MOST high, almighty Lord God,
To You belong praise, glory, honor and all blessings.

Praise to my Lord God with all His creatures,
And especially our brother the sun, who brings us the day
    and who brings us the light;

Fair is he who shines with such great splendor;
O Lord, he signifies You to us!

Praise to my Lord for our sister the moon and for the
    stars,
Which He has set clear and lovely in heaven.

Praise to my Lord for our brother the wind, for air and
    clouds, calms and all weather
By which You sustain life in all creatures.

Praise to my Lord for all those who pardon one another for
    His love's sake,
And who endure weakness and tribulation;

Blessed are they who peaceably shall endure;
For You, O God, shall give them a crown!

Praise to my Lord for our sister, the death of the body
    from which no man escapes.
Woe to him who dies in mortal sin!

Blessed are they who are found walking in Your most holy
    will,
For the second death shall have no power to do them
    harm.

Praise and bless the Lord and give Him thanks,
And serve Him with great humility.

St. Edmund (c. 1190 - 1240) was the Archbishop of Canterbury for a short period of time. Most of his life was spent in preaching and teaching. Feast: November 16.

INTO Your hands, O Lord, and into the hands of Your Holy Angels, I commit and entrust this day my soul, my relations, my benefactors, my friends and my enemies and all Your Catholic people.

Keep us, O Lord, through the day, by the merits and intercession of the Blessed Virgin Mary and all Your saints, from all vicious and unruly desires, from all sins and temptations of the devil, and from sudden and unprovided death and the pains of hell.

Illuminate my heart with the grace of the Holy Spirit; grant that I may ever be obedient to Your commandments; suffer me not to be separated from You, O God, who live and reign with God the Father and the same Holy Spirit for ever and ever. Amen.

St. Clare of Assisi (1194 - 1253) was the Foundress of the Poor Clares. She faithfully followed the rules drawn up by St. Francis of Assisi. Feast: August 11.

PRAISE and glory be to You, O loving Jesus Christ, for the most sacred wound in Your side, and by that adorable wound and by Your infinite mercy which You made known to us in the opening of Your breast to the soldier Longinus, and so to us all.

I pray You, O most gentle Jesus, having redeemed me by baptism from original sin, so now by Your Precious Blood, which is offered and received throughout the world, deliver me from all evils, past, present and to come.

And, by Your most bitter death give me a lively faith, a firm hope and a perfect charity, so that I may love You with all my heart and all my soul and all my strength; make me firm and steadfast in good works and grant me perseverance in Your service, so that I may be able to please You always. Amen.

St. Anthony of Padua, a Portuguese, was the first theologian for the Franciscan Order (1195 - 1231). He has been called the Evangelical Doctor. Feast: June 13.

OUR holy Lady, glorious Mother of God,
  The Queen of Heaven and our struggling race,
Exalted high above angelic choirs,
  Fill up the vessel of our heart with grace.

With wisdom's purest gold enrich our hearts,
  And make them strong, intrepid with your might;
Bedeck them with your precious virtues all,
  Which gleam with shining jewels, dazzling bright.

Blest Olive Tree, endued with fruit by God,
  Pour out on us the balm of mercy's oil,
That we may pardon find and reach our goal,
  In bliss forever, after trial and toil.

May Jesus Christ, your Son, this favor grant,
  For He made you over angel hosts to reign,
And crowned you with a royal diadem,
  Enthroned you as the Queen of Heaven's domain.

St. Richard of Chichester was an English bishop during the troubled times of King Henry III (c. 1197 - 1253). He was a pastoral bishop of great generosity. Feast: April 3.

THANKS be to You, My Lord Jesus Christ, for all the blessings and benefits which You have given me, for all the pains and insults You have borne for me.

O Most merciful Friend, my Brother and Redeemer, may I know You more clearly, love You more dearly, and follow You more nearly, day by day, day by day. Amen.

St. Albert the Great was a German Dominican and a bishop (c. 1200 - 1280). He had a decisive influence over the mind of his star pupil, St. Thomas Aquinas. He is called the Universal Doctor. Feast: November 15.

"FEAR not, Mary, for you have found grace with God" (Luke 1:30). Fear not, Mary for you have found, not taken grace, as Lucifer tried to take it.

You have not lost it as Adam lost it. You have found it because you desired it and sought after it. You have found uncreated grace: that is, God himself became your Son, and with that grace you have found and obtained every uncreated good. Amen.

St. Bonaventure was the great Franciscan cardinal-bishop in Albano, outside of Rome (c. 1217 - 1274). He was famous for his scriptural writings and his life of St. Francis of Assisi. He is called the Seraphic Doctor. Feast: July 15.

O MOST holy virgin, Mother of Our Lord Jesus Christ: by the overwhelming grief you experienced when you witnessed the martyrdom, the crucifixion, and the death of your divine Son, look upon me with eyes of compassion and awaken in my heart a tender commiseration for those sufferings, as well as a sincere detestation of my sins, in order that, being disengaged from all undue affection for the passing joys of this earth, I may long for the eternal Jerusalem, and that henceforth all my thoughts and all my actions may be directed toward this one most desirable object.

Honor, glory and love to our divine Lord Jesus, and to the holy and immaculate Mother of God. Amen.

O HOLY Lord, Father Almighty, everlasting God, for Your sake and that of Your Son who suffered and died for me; through the merits of the Virgin Mary and all the saints, grant that I may love You above all else, acknowledging my unworthiness and complaining of nothing but my faults. Amen.

PENETRATE me, O Lord Jesus, to the bottom of my heart with the sweet and salutary wound of Your love. Fill me with that ardent, sincere and tranquil love which caused Your apostle St. Paul to desire that he might be separated from his body to be with You.

May my soul languish for You, filled incessantly with

the desire for Your eternal dwelling. May I hunger for You, the Bread of Angels, the food of holy souls, the living Bread we should eat every day, the nourishing Bread which sustains the hearts of men and women and contains in itself all sweetness.

May my heart always hunger for You, O most desirable Bread, and feed on You without ceasing. May I thirst for You, O fountain of life, living source of wisdom and knowledge, torrent of delight which rejoices and refreshes the house of God. May I never cease to long for You whom the angels desire to see, whom they behold always with fresh ardor.

May my soul desire You, may it seek You, may it find You, may it tend to You, may it reach You. Be the object of my desires, the subject of my meditations and colloquies. May I do all things for Your glory and humility, consideration, prudence and discretion, with love and joy and perseverance enduring to the end.

And be, yourself alone, my hope, my trust, my riches, my pleasure, my joy, my rest, my tranquility, the peace of my soul. Draw me to Your sweetness, Your perfume, Your sweet savor; be to me a solid and pleasant nourishment.

May I love You, may I serve You without distaste and without relaxing in fervor. Be my refuge, my consolation, my help and my strength. And be my wisdom, my portion, my good, my treasure, wherein my heart may always be — and may my soul remain eternally, firmly and immovably rooted in You alone. Amen.

LET those who seek for miracles invoke the glorious St. Anthony. At his word all evils disappear, death and error, demons and leprosy; the sick rise up restored to perfect health.

His word and presence calm the troubled seas and

break the captive's chain, lost things are found, and old and young never appeal to him in vain. Perils are averted, hostilities cease.

If proof be needed of the truth of this, listen to the testimony of the people of Padua, eyewitnesses to these wondrous deeds.

St. Anthony of Padua, pray for us.

St. Thomas Aquinas was the great Dominican writer (1225 - 1274) who gave us the *Summa Theologiae*. He has been called Doctor Angelicus, Doctor Communis and the Great Synthesizer. Feast: January 28.

THE Cross is my sure salvation.
The Cross it is that I honor evermore.
The Cross of Our Lord is with me.
The Cross is my refuge.

GRANT me to impart willingly to others whatever I possess that is good and to ask humbly of others that I may partake of the good of which I am destitute: to confess truly my faults; to bear with equanimity the pains and evils which I suffer. Grant that I may never envy the good of my neighbor and that I may always return thanks for Your graces.

Let me always observe discipline in my clothing, movements and gestures. Let my tongue be restrained from vain words, my feet from going astray, my eyes from seeking after vain objects, my ears from listening to much news; may I humbly incline my face and raise my spirit to heaven.

Grant me to despise all transitory things and to desire You alone; to subdue my flesh and purify my conscience; to honor Your saints and to praise You worthily; to advance in virtue and to end good actions by a happy death.

Plant in me, O Lord, all virtues: that I may be devoted to divine things, provident in human affairs and troublesome to no one in bodily cares.

Grant me, O Lord, fervor in contrition, sincerity in confession and completeness in satisfaction for sins.

Deign to direct my soul to a good life: that what I do

may be pleasing to You, meritorious for myself and edifying to my neighbor.

Grant that I may never desire to do what is foolish and that I may never be discouraged by what is distasteful; and that I may never begin my works before the proper time, nor abandon them before they are completed. Amen.

GRANT me grace, O merciful God, to desire ardently all that is pleasing to You, to examine it prudently, to acknowledge it truthfully and to accomplish it perfectly for the praise and glory of Your name. Amen.

O MARY, Mother of fair love, of fear, of knowledge and of holy hope, by whose loving care and intercession many otherwise poor in intellect have wonderfully advanced in knowledge and holiness, I choose you as the guide and patroness of my studies; and I humbly implore, through the deep tenderness of your maternal love, and especially through the eternal Wisdom who deigned to take our flesh from you and who gifted you beyond all the saints with heavenly light, that you would obtain for me, by your intercession, the grace of the Holy Spirit that I may be able to grasp with strong intellect, retain in memory, proclaim by word and deed, and teach others all things which bring honor to you and to your Son, and which for me and for others are salutary for eternal life. Amen.

O GOOD Jesus, I know that every perfect gift and, above all others, that of chastity depends on the powerful action of Your divine Providence; I know that without You, a creature can do nothing.

This is why I beg You to defend, by Your grace, the purity of my soul and of my body. And, if I have ever received any impression whatsoever of a sentiment capable of soiling this ineffable virtue, O Supreme Master of my faculties, blot it out from my soul, that with a clean heart I may advance in Your love and in Your service, offering myself chaste all the days of my life on the most pure altar of Your divinity.

It is the Cross that I cherish. The Cross of the Lord is with me. The Cross is my refuge. Amen.

These five Eucharistic hymns by St. Thomas witness the deep mystical flavor of prayer-life in the thirteenth century. More of this can be studied in William Thomas Walsh's *Thirteenth, Greatest of Centuries.*

Lauda Sion Salvatorem

PRAISE, O Sion, praise Your Savior,
Shepherd, Prince, with glad behavior,
   Praise in hymn and canticle.
Sing His glory without measure,
For the merit of your treasure
   Never shall your praises fill.

Wondrous theme of mortal singing
Living Bread and Bread life-bringing,
   Sing we on this joyful day:
At the Lord's own table given
To the Twelve as Bread from Heaven,
   Doubting not, we firmly say.

Sing His praise with voice sonorous;
Every heart shall hear the chorus
   Swell in melody sublime:
For this day the Shepherd gave us

Flesh and blood to feed and save us
　Lasting to the end of time.

At the new King's sacred table,
The new Law's new Pasch is able
　To succeed the ancient Rite.
Old to new its place has given,
Truth has far the shadows driven,
　Darkness flees before the Light.

And as He has done and planned it —
"Do this" — hear His love command it,
　"For a memory of Me."
Learned Lord, in Your own science.
Bread and wine in sweet compliance
　As a Host we offer thee.

Thus in faith the Christian hears
That Christ's Flesh as Bread appears,
　And as wine His Precious Blood.
Though we feel it not nor see it,
Living Faith that does decree it
　All defects of sense makes good.

Lo! beneath the species dual —
Signs, not things — is hid a jewel
　Far beyond creation's reach.
Though His Flesh as food abides,
And His Blood as drink — he hides
　Undivided under each.

Whosoever eats can never
Break the Body, rend or sever;
　Christ entire fills our hearts:
Thousands eat the Bread of Heaven,
Yet as much to one is given:

Christ, though eaten, still remains

Good and bad, they come to greet Him:
Unto life the former eat Him,
    And the latter unto death;
These find death and those find heaven;
See, from the same life-seed given,
    How the harvest differeth.

When at last the Bread is broken,
Doubt not what the Lord has spoken;
In each part the same love-token,
    The same Christ our hearts adore:
For no power the Thing divides —
'Tis the symbols He provides,
While the Savior still abides,
    Undiminished as before.

Hail, the angelic Bread of Heaven,
Now the pilgrim's hoping-leaven,
Yea, the Bread to children given
    That to dogs must not be thrown:
In the figures contemplated,
'Twas with Isaac immolated;
By the Lamb 'twas antedated;
    In the Manna it was known.

O Good Shepherd, still confessing
Love, in spite of our transgressing —
Here Your blessed Food processing,
Make us share Your every blessing
    In the land of life and love:
You, whose power has all completed
And Your Flesh as Food has meted,
Make us at Your table seated
By Your saints, as friends be greeted,

In Your paradise above.

Pange Lingua

SING, my tongue, the Savior's glory,
  Of His Flesh the mystery sing;
Of the Blood, all price exceeding,
  Shed by our immortal King,
Destined for the world's redemption,
  From a noble womb to spring.

Of a pure and spotless Virgin
  Born for us on earth below,
He, as Man, with man conversing,
  Stayed, the seeds of truth to sow;
Then he closed the solemn order
  Wondrously His life of woe.

On the night of that Last Supper
  Seated with His chosen band,
He the Paschal Victim eating,
  First fulfills the Law's command:
Then as food to all His brethren
  Gives himself with His own hand.

Word made Flesh, the bread of nature
  By His word to Flesh He turns;
Wine into His Blood He changes:
  What though sense no change discerns?
Only be the heart in earnest,
  Faith her lesson quickly learns.

(Tantum Ergo)

DOWN in adoration falling,
  Lo! the Sacred Host we hail;

Lo! O'er ancient forms departing,
   Newer rites of grace prevail;
Faith for all defects supplying
   Where the feeble senses fail.

To the everlasting Father,
   And the Son who reigns on high,
With the Holy Spirit proceeding
   Forth from Each eternally,
Be salvation, honor, blessing,
   Might and endless majesty.

Sacris Solemniis Juncta Sint Gaudia

AT this our solemn Feast
   Let holy joys abound,
And from the inmost breast
   Let songs of praise resound;
Let ancient rites depart
   And all be new around,
In every act and voice and heart.

Remember we that eve,
   When the Last Supper spread,
Christ, as we all believe,
   The lamb, with leavenless bread,
Among His brethren shared,
   And thus the Law obeyed,
Of old unto their sires declared.

The typic lamb consumed,
   The regal Feast complete,
The Lord unto the Twelve
   His Body gave to eat;
The whole to all, no less

The whole to each, did mete
With His own hands, as we confess.

He gave them, weak and frail,
  His Flesh, their food to be;
On them, downcast and sad,
  His Blood bestowed He:
And thus to them He spake,
  "Receive this cup from Me,
And all of you of this partake."

So He this Sacrifice
  To institute did will,
And charged His priests alone
  That office to fulfill:
In them He did confide:
  To whom it still pertains
To take, and to the rest divide.

(Panis Angelicus)

THIS Angel's Bread is made
  The Bread of man today:
The Living Bread from Heaven
  With figures does away:
O wondrous gift indeed!
  The poor and lowly may
Upon their Lord and Master feed.

O Triune Deity,
  To You we meekly pray,
So You may visit us,
  As we our homage pay;
And in Your footsteps bright
  Conduct us on our way
To where You dwell in cloudless light.

Verbum Supernum Prodiens

THE Heavenly Word proceeding forth,
  Yet leaving not the Father's side,
And going to His work on earth
  Had reached at length life's eventide.

By false disciple to be given
  To foemen for His Blood athirst,
Himself, the Living Bread from Heaven,
  He gave to His disciples first.

To them He gave, in twofold kind,
  His very Flesh, His very Blood:
In love's own fulness thus designed
  Of the whole man to be the food.

By birth, our fellow man was He;
  Our meat, while sitting at the board,
He died our ransomer to be;
  He ever reigns, our great reward.

(O Salutaris Hostia)

O saving Victim, opening wide,
  The gate of heaven to man below,
Our foes press on from every side
  Your aid supply, Your strength bestow.

To Your great Name be endless praise,
  Immortal Godhead, One in Three.
O grant us endless length of days
  In our true native land with thee.

Adoro Te Devote

HIDDEN God, devoutly I adore You,
   Truly present underneath these veils;
All my heart subdues itself before You,
   Since to fathom You it faints and fails.

Not to sight or taste or touch be credit,
   Hearing only do we trust secure;
I believe, for God the Son has said it —
   Word of truth that ever shall endure.

On the Cross was veiled the Godhead's splendor,
   Here Your humanness lies hidden, too;
Unto both alike my faith I render,
   And, as sued the contrite thief, I sue.

Though I look not on Your wounds like Thomas,
   You, my Lord, and You, My God, I call;
Make me more and more believe Your promise,
   Hope in You and love You over all.

O Memorial of my Savior dying,
   Living Bread, imparting life to man;
May my soul, its life from You supplying,
   Taste Your sweetness, as on earth it can.

Deign, O Jesus, Pelican of heaven,
   Me, a sinner, in Your Blood to lave,
To a single drop of which is given
   All the world from all its sin to save.

Contemplating, Lord, Your hidden presence,
   Grant me what I thirst for and implore,
In the revelation of Your essence
   To behold Your glory evermore.

O SACRED Banquet, in which Christ is received, the memory of His Passion is recalled, the soul is filled with Grace, and there is given to us the pledge of future glory!

O Jesus our Good Shepherd, Living Bread, have mercy on us; feed and guide us; grant that we may see the good things in the land of the living.

You who know all things and can do all things, You who feed us mortals here below, let us share one day in Your banquet as co-heirs and partners of Your saints. Amen.

Blessed Jacopone da Todi was caught up in all the political intrigue of his times (1230 - 1306). In the midst of his many exiles and imprisonments, he is credited with writing the *Stabat Mater*. Feast: December 25.

At the Cross her station keeping
Stood the mournful Mother weeping,
　　Close to Jesus at the last.

Through her heart, His sorrow sharing,
All His bitter anguish bearing,
　　Lo! the piercing sword had passed.

O how sad and sore distressed
Was that Mother, highly blessed,
　　Of the sole-begotten One.

Woebegone, with heart's prostration,
Mother meek, the bitter Passion
　　Saw she of her glorious Son.

Who on Christ's dear Mother gazing,
In her trouble so amazing,
　　Born of woman, would not weep?

Who on Christ's dear Mother thinking,
Such a cup of sorrow drinking,
　　Would not share her sorrow deep?

For His people's sins rejected,
Saw her Jesus unprotected.
　　Saw with thorns, with scourges rent;

Saw her Son from judgment taken,
Her Beloved in death forsaken,

Till His spirit forth He sent.

Fount of love and holy sorrow,
Mother, may my spirit borrow
  Somewhat of your woe profound.

Unto Christ with pure emotion,
Raise my contrite heart's devotion,
  Love to read in every wound.

Those five wounds on Jesus smitten,
Mother! in my heart be written,
  Deep as in your own they be.

You, your Savior's Cross did bare,
You, your Son's rebuke did share.
  Let me share them both with thee.

In the passion of my Maker,
Be my sinful soul partaker,
  Weep 'til death and weep with you.

Mine with you be that sad station,
There to watch the great salvation,
  Wrought upon th' atoning Tree.

Virgin, you of virgins fairest,
May the bitter woe thou bearest
  Make on me impression deep.

Thus Christ's dying may I carry,
With Him in His Passion tarry,
  And His wounds in memory keep.

May His wound both wound and heal me,
He enkindle, cleanse, anneal me,

By His Cross my hope and stay.

May He, when the mountains quiver,
From that flame which burns forever,
    Shield me on the Judgment Day.

Jesus, may Your Cross defend me,
And Your Mother's prayer befriend me;
    Let me die in Your embrace.

When to dust my dust returns,
Grant a soul, that to You yearns,
    In Your paradise a place. Amen.

St. Gertrude the Great was a Cistercian nun (1257 -1302). She was favored with many private revelations and she had great devotion to the Blessed Sacrament and to the Sacred Heart of Jesus, long before this was so popular. Feast: November 16.

I SALUTE you through the Heart of Jesus, O all you holy angels and saints of God; I rejoice in your glory and I give thanks to Our Lord for all the benefits which He has showered upon you.

I praise Him and glorify Him, and offer you, for an increase of your joy and honor, the most gentle Heart of Jesus. Deign, therefore, to pray for me that I may become according to the heart of God. Amen.

O ALMIGHTY and everlasting God, seeing that it is the true faith of Your Church that the holy sacrifice of the Mass instituted by Your Son is infinitely pleasing to Your divine Majesty, and renders to You an infinite worship and praise, and since by it alone can You be worthily and adequately worshiped and praised; impelled by an ardent desire for Your honor and glory, I purpose to assist at this present Sacrifice with the utmost devotion of which I am capable, and to offer this holy Oblation to You in union with Your priest.

I offer You not only this Sacrifice, but all those which shall be offered up this day from every part of the world. I implore You, O most holy Father, through Jesus Christ, Your Son, to pour into the hearts of all Your priests the spirit of grace and fervor. May they always celebrate Your tremendous Mystery with becoming awe and devotion.

Grant to me and to all those who are here present with me that we may join in this most sacred action with reverence and devotion so that we may have our portion in its fruit and effect.

I confess to You, O almighty God, and to the Blessed Mary ever Virgin, and to all the saints, my own sins and those of the world; and I lay them on Your sacred altar that they may be utterly blotted out by the virtue of this Sacrifice. Grant us this grace by that love which held back Your hand from striking when Your most beloved Son, Your only Son, was immolated by the hands of ungodly men. Amen.

O SACRED Heart of Jesus! living and life-giving fountain of eternal life, infinite treasure of the divinity, glowing furnace of love. You are my refuge and my sanctuary.

O my adorable and lovely Savior! consume my heart with that burning fire wherewith Yours is ever inflamed; pour down on my soul those graces which flow from Your love, and let my heart be so united with Yours that our wills may be one, mine conformed to Yours in all things.

May Your will be the rule alike of my desires and my actions. Amen.

(This prayer is also attributed to St. Mechthild, a contemporary of St. Gertrude's:)

I ADORE and praise and bless You, O Lord Jesus Christ, giving thanks for the love and confidence with which You overcame death, rose from the tomb, and thus restored dignity and glory to our humanity.

Ascending into heaven You have been seated at the right hand of God. There I beseech You on behalf of the souls for which I pray. Make them sharers in Your glory, in Your victory. Amen.

St. Simon Stock was a Carmelite who became famous for promoting the Brown Scapular (died 1265). Under his direction the Carmelites spread throughout Europe. Feast: May 16.

O BEAUTIFUL Flower of Carmel, most fruitful vine, Splendor of Heaven, holy and singular, who brought forth the Son of God, still ever remaining a pure virgin, assist me in this necessity.

O Star of the Sea, help and protect me! Show me that you are my Mother. Amen.

St. Bridget of Sweden was a mystic, a religious founder and a widow (1303 - 1373). In her *Revelationes* she reports on many private visions she received. She wrote fifteen famous prayers; this is the first of them. Feast: July 23.

OUR Father! Hail Mary! Oh, Jesus Christ! Eternal sweetness to those who love You, joy surpassing all joy and all desire, Salvation and hope of all sinners, You have no greater desire than to be among mankind, even assuming human nature at the fullness of time for love of us; recall all the sufferings You endured from the instant of Your conception, and especially during Your Passion, as was decreed and ordained from all eternity in the divine plan.

Remember, O Lord, that during the Last Supper with Your disciples, having washed their feet, You gave them Your Most Precious Body and Blood and at the same time that You consoled them, You foretold Your coming Passion.

Remember the sadness and bitterness You experienced in Your soul as You bore witness saying, "My Soul is sorrowful even unto death."

Remember all the fear, anguish and pain that You suffered in Your delicate Body before the torment of the Crucifixion when, after having prayed three times, bathed in a sweat of blood, You were betrayed by Judas, Your disciple, arrested by the people of a nation You had chosen and elevated, accused by false witnesses, unjustly judged by three judges during the flower of Your youth, during the solemn Paschal season.

Remember that You were stripped of Your garments and clothed in those of derision, that Your face and eyes were veiled, that You were struck, crowned with thorns, a reed placed in Your hands and that You were crushed with blows and overwhelmed with affronts and outrages.

In memory of these pains and sufferings which You endured before Your Passion on the Cross, grant me before my death true contrition, a sincere and entire confession, worthy satisfaction and the remission of all my sins. Amen.

Blessed Henry Susa (c. 1310 - 1365) was a mystic and a disciple of Meister Eckhart. He wrote several devotional works. Feast: March 2.

O CHOSEN Queen, you are the gate of all grace, the door of compassion that is never shut. Heaven and earth may pass away before you will permit anyone who earnestly seeks your help to depart from you without obtaining it.

For this very reason you are the first object my soul sees when I awake, the last when I lie down to sleep. How should anything which your pure hands present before God and commend to Him be rejected, small though it be?

St. Catherine of Siena was the second woman to be named a Doctor of the Church (c. 1347 - 1380). She was a mystic who authored many learned books on prayer and spirituality. Feast: April 29.

MY sweet Lord, look with mercy upon Your people and especially upon the Church, Your mystical Body. Do not let sin darken the life of Your Church, Your holy Bride.

Moved by love and wishing to reconcile the human race to Yourself, You gave us Your only-begotten Son. He became our Mediator and our justice by taking on all our injustice and sin out of obedience to Your will, eternal Father, just as You willed that He take on our human nature. What an immeasurably profound love!

Your Son went down from the heights of His divinity to the depths of our humanity. Can anyone's heart remain closed and hardened after this?

We image Your divinity, but You image our humanity in that union of the two which You have worked in a man. You have veiled the Godhead in a cloud, in the clay of our humanity.

Only Your love could so dignify the flesh of Adam. And so by reason of this immeasurable love I beg, with all my strength, that You freely extend Your mercy to all your lowly creatures.

ETERNAL God, eternal Trinity, You have made the Blood of Christ so precious through His sharing in Your divine nature. You are a mystery as deep as the sea; the more I search, the more I find, and the more I find the more I search for You.

I can never be satisfied; what I receive will ever leave me desiring more. When You fill my soul I have an even greater hunger and I grow more famished for Your light. I desire above all else to see You, the true light, as You really are.

You are my Creator, Eternal Trinity, and I am Your creature. You have made me a new creation in the blood of Your Son, and I know that You are moved with love at the beauty of Your creation.

I know that You are beauty and wisdom itself. The food of angels, You gave Yourself to us in the fire of Your love, O Triune God!

O TENDER Father, You gave me more, much more than I ever thought to ask for. I realize that our human desires can never really match what You long to give us.

Thanks, and again thanks, O Father, for having granted my petitions, and that which I never realized I needed or petitioned. Amen.

St. Vincent Ferrer was a Spanish Dominican (1350 - 1418). He was noted for his fine sermons. Feast: April 5.

LORD Jesus Christ, who wills that no one should perish and to whom supplication is never made without the hope of mercy — for You said with Your own holy and blessed lips: All things whatsoever you ask in My name will be done to you — I ask You, O Lord, for the sake of Your holy name, to grant me at the hour of death full consciousness and the power of speech, sincere contrition for my sins, true faith, firm hope and perfect charity, that I may be able to say to You with a clean heart: Into Your hands, O Lord, I commend my spirit.

You have redeemed me, O God of truth, You who are blessed forever. Amen.

HAVE mercy on me, O Lord, for I am weak. Help me, O Lord, for my bones are troubled. My soul is troubled exceedingly. But You, O Lord, how long? Turn to me, O Lord, and deliver my soul.

O save me for Your mercy's sake. Have mercy on me O Lord; see my humiliation which I suffer from my enemies, You who lift me up from the gates of death, that I may declare all Your praises in the gates of the daughter of Zion.

Have mercy on me, O Lord, for I am afflicted.

Have mercy on me, O God, according to Your great mercy; and according to the multitude of Your tender mercies, blot out my iniquity.

Have mercy on me, O God, have mercy on me, for my soul trusts in You. In the shadow of Your wings I will hope until iniquity pass away. I will cry to God the Most High, to God who has done so many good things for me.

Have mercy on me, O Lord; for I have cried to You all the day long. Give joy to the soul of Your servant; for to You O Lord I have lifted up my soul. You, O Lord, are sweet and mild, plenteous in mercy to all who call upon You.

St. Bernardine of Siena was an Italian Franciscan who was a noted preacher (1380 - 1444). He had a very special devotion to the Holy Name of Jesus. Feast: May 20.

BE mindful of us, O blessed Joseph, and intercede for us with your foster-Son by pleading for us. Also ask the Blessed Virgin Mary, your spouse, that she intercede for us, for she is the Mother of Him who, with the Father and the Holy Spirit, lives and reigns world without end. Amen.

JESUS, Name full of glory, grace, love and strength! You are the refuge of those who repent, our banner of warfare in this life, the medicine of souls, the comfort of those who mourn, the delight of those who believe, the light of those who preach the true faith, the wages of those who toil, the healing of the sick.

To You our devotion aspires; by You our prayers are received; we delight in contemplating You. O Name of Jesus, You are the glory of all the saints for eternity. Amen.

Blessed Alan de la Roche was a French Dominican who gave us the Rosary of the Blessed Mother in its modern form (c. 1425 - 1475). He modestly attributed his work to St. Dominic, but the best scholarship demonstrates that Blessed Alan's life work was the promotion of this particular Marian devotion (feast: Oct. 7).

He took the 150 Hail Mary's in imitation of the 150 Psalms and divided them into decades, separated by an Our Father. The Doxology was added to the end of each decade. Decades were probably chosen since they could be counted on the two hands.

The 150 prayers were divided into three groupings of five decades each. Blessed Alan named them and divided them as follows:

JOYFUL Mysteries — The Annunciation
                   The Visitation
                   The Nativity
                   The Presentation
                   Finding the Child in the Temple

SORROWFUL Mysteries — The Agony in the Garden
                      The Scourging at the Pillar
                      The Crowning with Thorns
                      The Carrying of the Cross
                      The Crucifixion

GLORIOUS Mysteries — The Resurrection
                     The Ascension
                     The Descent of the Holy
                        Spirit at Pentecost
                     The Assumption of Mary
                        into Heaven

The Coronation of Our Lady,
Queen of Heaven and Earth.

(Various prayers may be added as introduction or conclusion, especially for an increase of faith, hope and
charity.)

IV

The Church on the Move

FOR almost a generation after Martin Luther's break with Rome, the Catholic theologians did not take his reforms seriously. They said that he and his followers were innovators, inventing doctrines that had never before been heard of in Christianity. In fact, the Latin name for the Reformation theologians was *innovatores*, the innovators.

But the Spirit was active, and many saints were raised up to carry on the work of the Catholic Counter-Reformation. Chief among them were St. Ignatius Loyola and his many Jesuit disciples.

Add to this the work of St. Teresa of Avila and her Carmelites and there is a whole new spiritual armada that rushed into the fray. St. Francis de Sales was another powerhouse.

St. Alphonsus, the great moral theologian, rounds out this section historically and prayerfully.

St. Joan of Valois (or of France) suffered terribly from family conflicts (1464 - 1505). After her marriage to Louis XII was annulled, she founded an order of nuns dedicated to the Annunciation. Feast: February 4.

Excerpts from "The Ten Virtues of Our Lady"

O VIRGIN most truthful, the soil from which, in the words of David, Truth sprang, grant us the grace to keep in all things truth of heart, of word and of deed.

O Virgin most patient, grant us patience amid the trials and sorrows so plentiful in this world, so that after the storm of adversities, afflictions and anguish, which everywhere assail us, we may with joy reach the land of the living, the haven of eternal beatitude, there to enjoy the everlasting rest prepared for the elect.

O Virgin most charitable, fill our hearts with charity, with love, and with God's grace. Mother of Mercy, under this dear title the Church invokes you, have pity on us, oppressed beneath the weight of our sins and afflictions. Look on us, in your maternal pity, that your mercy may lead you to help us in our needs.

St. Thomas More was the chancellor of the English kingdom under Henry VIII (1478 - 1535). He was martyred because he refused to renounce the authority of the popes. Feast: June 22.

GIVE me the grace, good Lord:

— To set the world at naught, to set the mind firmly on You and not to hang upon the words of men's mouths;

— To be content to be solitary; not to long for worldly pleasures; little by little, utterly to cast off the world and rid my mind of all its business;

— Not to long to hear of earthly things, but that the hearing of worldly fancies may be displeasing to me;

— Gladly to be thinking of God, piteously to call for His help; to lean into the comfort of God; busily to labor to love Him.

— To know my own vileness and wretchedness; to humble myself under the mighty hand of God; to bewail my sins and, for the purging of them, patiently to suffer adversity.

— Gladly to bear my purgatory here; to be joyful in tribulations; to walk the narrow way that leads to life.

— To have the last thing in remembrance; to have ever before my eyes my death that is ever at hand; to make death no stranger to me; to foresee and consider the everlasting fire of hell; to pray for pardon before the judge comes.

— To have continually in mind the passion that Christ suffered for me; for His benefits unceasingly to give Him thanks.

— To buy the time again that I have lost. To abstain from vain conversations, to shun foolish mirth and gladness; to cut off unnecessary recreations.

— Of worldly substance, friends, liberty, life and all, to set the loss at naught, for the winning of Christ.

— To think my worst enemies my best friends, for the brethren of Joseph could never have done him so much good with their love and favor as they did him with their malice and hatred.

These minds are more to be desired of every man than all the treasures of all the princes and kings, Christian and heathen, were it gathered and laid together all in one heap. Amen.

(The prayer above was composed in the Tower of London in the time preceding his beheading.)

ALMIGHTY God, have mercy on N_____ and on all that bear me evil will and would do me harm, and on their faults and mine together, by such easy, tender, merciful means as Your infinite wisdom can best devise.

Grant us amendment and redress and make us saved souls together, where we may ever live and love together with You and all Your blessed saints, O glorious Trinity, for the bitter Passion of our Savior Christ. Amen.

St. Ignatius Loyola (c. 1491 - 1556) founded the Society of Jesus. He is most famous for his *Spiritual Exercises*. Feast: July 31.

TEACH us, good Lord, to serve You as You deserve; to give and not to count the cost; to fight and not to heed the wounds; to toil and not to seek for rest; to labor and not to ask for any reward, save that of knowing that we do Your will.

TAKE, O Lord, and receive my entire liberty, my memory, my understanding and my whole will. All that I am, all that I have, You have given me, and I will give it back to You to be disposed of according to Your good pleasure.

Give me only Your love and Your grace; with You I am rich enough, nor do I ask for anything besides.

BEHOLD, O supreme King and Lord of all, I, though most unworthy, yet relying on Your grace and help, offer myself entirely to You, and submit all that I have to Your will, declaring before Your infinite goodness, and in the sight of the glorious Virgin, Your Mother, and all the heavenly court, that this is my mind, my desire and my decree: to follow You as nearly as I can, and to imitate You in bearing insults and adversities with true patience, both interior and exterior. Amen.

(St. Ignatius' favorite prayer:)

Anima Christi

SOUL of Christ sanctify me;
Body of Christ, save me;
Blood of Christ, inebriate me;
Water from the side of Christ, wash me;
Passion of Christ, strengthen me;
O Good Jesus, hear me;
Within Your wounds, hide me;
Never permit me to be separated from You;
From the wicked enemy, defend me;
In the hour of my death, call me
And bid me to come to Your side,
That with Your saints I may praise You,
For ever and ever. Amen.

*(This prayer is attributed, by some,
to Blessed Bernardine of Feltran.)*

Pope St. Pius V was the energetic Dominican pope who was a hero of the Counter-Reformation (1504 - 1672). He vigorously enforced the decrees of the Council of Trent. Feast: April 30.

JESUS Christ Crucified, Son of the most holy Virgin Mary! Incline Your sacred head and listen to my petitions and sighs, as You listened to Your eternal Father on Mt. Thabor.

Jesus Christ Crucified, Son of the most holy Virgin Mary! Open Your sacred eyes and look on me as You looked on Your holy Mother from the cross.

Jesus Christ Crucified, son of the most holy Virgin Mary! Open Your sacred lips and speak to my afflicted heart, as You spoke to St. John, to whom You commended Your dear Mother.

Jesus Christ Crucified, Son of the most holy Virgin Mary! Open Your sacred arms and receive me, Your poor child, as You embraced the hard wood of the cross for love of me and all sinners.

Lord Jesus Christ crucified, Son of the most holy Virgin Mary! Open Your Sacred Heart, that seat of love and mercy, and receive mine into it; make it wholly Yours. Hear my prayers and grant my petitions.

St. Francis Xavier was a Spanish Jesuit who conducted extensive missions in the Far East (1506 - 1552). He was among the first of the Jesuits, recruited by St. Ignatius Loyola. Feast: December 3.

O MY Lord Jesus! Teach me to be generous; teach me to serve You as You deserve; to give and not to count the cost; to fight and not to heed the wounds; to toil and not to ask for rest; to labor, seeking no reward, save that of knowing that I do Your will. Amen.

O ETERNAL God, Creator of all things, remember the infidel peoples whom You have created in Your own image and likeness. Bear in mind that Your Son Jesus suffered a most cruel death for their salvation.

Lord, do not permit Your Son to be despised by infidels, but be appeased by the prayers of Your saints and the Church, the Spouse of Your most holy Son. Remember Your mercy and blot out idolatry and infidelity. May these people be ignorant no longer of Him who is our salvation, life and resurrection, through whom we have been saved and liberated. To Him let there be glory throughout all ages. Amen.

O GOD, You are the object of my love,
Not for the hope of endless joys above,
Nor for the fear of endless pains below,
Which those who love You not must undergo.

For me and such as me, You once did bear
The ignominious cross, the nails, the spear:
A thorny crown transpierced Your sacred brow;

What bloody sweats from every member flow.

Such as then was and is Your love for me,
Such is and shall be still my love for Thee;
Your love, O Jesus, will I ever sing —
O God of love, sweet Savior, dearest King!

St. Teresa of Avila (1515 - 1582) is one of only two women who have been declared "Doctors of the Church." She was a Spanish Carmelite who wrote admirable books about prayer and mystical theology. Feast: October 15.

O SON of the eternal Father, Jesus Christ, our Lord and King of all. What have You left behind You in the world, that we, as Your heirs, could inherit from You?

What did You possess but sorrow, pain, ignominy and a tree on which You suffered a most bitter death?

We, Your true children, O God, will not abandon our inheritance; we shall not flee from suffering. Amen.

LORD, grant that I may always allow myself to be guided by You, always follow Your plans and perfectly accomplish Your holy will.

Grant that in all things, great and small, today and all the days of my life, I may do whatever You require of me. Help me respond to the slightest prompting of Your grace so that I may be Your trustworthy instrument for Your honor.

May Your will be done in time and in eternity — by me, in me and through me. Amen.

MY God, because You are so good, I love You with all my heart, and for Your sake I love my neighbor as myself.

If I love You, Lord, it is not just because of heaven which You have promised; if I fear to offend You, it is not because hell threatens me.

What draws me to you, O Lord, is Yourself alone, it is the sight of You, nailed to the cross for me, Your body bruised in the pains of death.

Your love so holds my heart that, if there were no heaven, I would love You still. If there were no hell I would even still fear to offend You.

I do not need Your gifts to make me love You, for even if I should have no help of hope at all of all the things I do hope for, I would still love You with that very same love. Amen.

CHRIST has no body now on earth, but yours,
   No hands but yours,
   No feet but yours.

Yours are the eyes through which the compassion of
      Christ
   must look out on the world.

Yours are the feet with which He is to go about
   doing good.

Yours are the hands with which He is to bless
   His people.

   LET nothing disturb you,
   Let nothing frighten you.
   All things pass.
   God does not change.
   Patience achieves everything.
   Whoever has God lacks nothing.
   God alone suffices.

St. Peter Canisius was a Dutch Jesuit and a very central figure in the Counter-Reformation (1521 - 1597). He was the author of some widely circulated catechisms. Feast: December 21.

O MY soul, why do you afflict me? O world, why do you oppress me? Never, never shall I abandon myself to you.

I trust in God, my Lord who sends me all for the best. I have been created and redeemed, not for the temporal, but for the eternal. Amen.

O GOD, the refuge of the poor, the strength of those who toil, and the Comforter of all who sorrow, we commend to Your mercy the unfortunate and the needy in whatever land they may be.

You alone know the number and extent of their sufferings and trials. Look down, Father of mercies, at those unhappy families suffering from war and slaughter, from hunger and illness and other severe troubles.

Spare them, O Lord, for it is truly a time of mercy. Amen.

St. Charles Borromeo (1538 - 1584) was the moving spirit behind the efforts to complete the Council of Trent. It was said that "the Holy Spirit traveled to Trent in the daily post sent from Cardinal Borromeo." Feast: November 4.

O HOLY Mother of God, pray for the priests Your Son has chosen to serve the Church. Help them, by your intercession, to be holy, zealous and chaste. Make them models of virtue in the service of God's people.

Help them be pious in meditation, efficacious in preaching and zealous in the daily offering of the Holy Sacrifice of the Mass. Help them administer the Sacraments with joy. Amen.

St. Paschal Baylon was a Spanish Franciscan lay-brother (1540 - 1692). He was a staunch defender of the doctrine of the Real Presence of Christ in the Blessed Sacrament. Feast: May 17.

I DESIRE to love You, my Lord, My Light
my Strength, my Deliverer, my God and my All.
What have I in heaven, O God, and what do I
want besides You on earth?
My spirit and my body languish with yearning for
Your Majesty.
You are the God of my heart, You are my portion,
my inheritance for eternity. Amen.

St. John of the Cross was one of the greatest mystical theologians (1542 - 1591). He was associated with St. Teresa of Avila in forming the Discalced Carmelites. He is called the Doctor of Mystical Theology. Feast: December 14.

O MY soul, set aside by grace, you are destined to be a partaker in the divine nature. Through this grace you are united to the Holy Trinity, not yet fully as in the life to come, but nonetheless even now in a real and perceptible way.

O my soul, created to enjoy such exquisite gifts, what are you doing, where are you going? How wretched is the blindness of Adam's children, if indeed we are blind to such a brilliant light and deaf to so insistent a voice!

St. Robert Bellarmine was a Jesuit and the Cardinal Archbishop of Capua (1542 - 1621). He was very active in the Counter-Reformation. Feast: September 17.

RULER of the dread immense!
　　Maker of this mighty frame!
Whose eternal providence
　　Guides it, as from You it came.

Low before Your throne we bend;
　　Hear our supplicating cries;
And Your light celestial send
　　With the freshly dawning skies.

King of kings and Lord most high!
　　This is Your dear love we pray:
May Your Guardian Angel nigh,
　　Keep us from all sin this day.

May he crush the deadly wiles
　　Of the envious serpent's art,
Ever spreading cunning toils
　　Round about the thoughtless heart

May he scatter ruthless war
　　Ere to this our land it come;
Plague and famine drive away
　　Fix securely peace at home.

Father, Son and Holy Spirit,
　　One eternal Unity
Guard by Your Angelic Host,
　　Us who put our trust in Thee. Amen.

St. John Leonardi of Lucca, Italy, founded the Clerks Regular of the Mother of God (1550 - 1609). He was an Italian priest who worked among prisoners. Feast: October 9.

ETERNAL God, behold me prostrate before Your immense majesty, humbly adoring You. I offer You all my thoughts, words and actions of this day.

I offer them all to be thought, spoken and done entirely for love of You, for Your glory, to fulfill Your divine will, to serve You, to praise You and bless You.

May they also be to my own enlightenment in the mysteries of the holy faith, for securing my salvation and the attainment of Your loving mercy. May they satisfy divine justice for my sins, in suffrage for the holy souls in purgatory and for the grace of a true conversion for all sinners.

I wish and intend to do everything in union with the most pure intentions of Jesus and Mary.

Receive, O my dearest God, my good intentions; give me Your blessing, with efficacious grace to keep me from mortal sins throughout all my life but particularly this day, on which I will to gain all the indulgences which I am capable of gaining, and to assist, were it possible, at all the Masses being celebrated throughout the world and offer them for all the souls in purgatory. Amen.

St. Joseph Calasanctius was a Spanish priest (1556 - 1648). He founded the Order of Pious Schools (Piarists). Feast: August 25.

LET us offer praise and thanksgiving to the Most Holy Trinity who has shown us the Virgin Mary, clothed with the sun, the moon beneath her feet, and on her head a mystic crown of twelve stars, for ever and ever. Amen.

Let us praise and thank the divine Father who elected her for His daughter. Amen. Our Father . . .

Praised be the divine Father who predestined her to be the Mother of His divine Son. Amen. Hail Mary . . .

Praised be the divine Father who preserved her from all stain in her conception. Amen. Hail Mary . . .

Praised be the divine Father who adorned her at her birth with His most excellent gifts. Amen. Hail Mary . . .

Praised be the divine Father who gave her St. Joseph to be her companion and most chaste spouse. Amen. Hail Mary . . . Glory be . . .

Let us praise and thank the divine Son who chose her for His Mother. Amen. Our Father . . .

Praised be the divine Son who became incarnate in her bosom and there abode for nine months. Amen. Hail Mary . . .

Praised be the divine Son who was born of her and was nourished at her breast. Amen. Hail Mary . . .

Praised be the divine Son who in His childhood willed to be taught by her. Amen. Hail Mary. . .

Praised be the divine Son who revealed to her the mystery of the redemption of the world. Amen. Hail Mary . . . Glory be . . .

Let us praise and thank the Holy Spirit who took her for His spouse. Amen. Our Father . . .

Praised be the Holy Spirit who revealed first to her His

name of Holy Spirit. Amen. Hail Mary . . .

Praised be the Holy Spirit by whose operation she was at once Virgin and Mother. Amen. Hail Mary . . .

Praised be the Holy Spirit by whose power she was the living temple of the ever-blessed Trinity. Amen. Hail Mary . . .

Praised be the Holy Spirit by whom she was exalted in heaven above every living creature. Amen. Hail Mary . . . Glory be . . .

St. Robert Southwell was an English Jesuit and a poet (1561 - 1595). He was martyred at Tyburn. Feast: February 21.

LOVE'S precious mark, highest theme of praise; most
　　desired light for man.
To love Him is life; to leave Him, death, to live in Him and
　　for Him, delight.
He is mine by gift; I am His by debt; thus each to the other
　　as meet.
He was my first friend; He is my best friend; all things
　　prove Him true.
Though young, He is wise; though small, He is strong; He
　　is both God and man.
As wise, He knows all; as strong, He can do all; as God,
　　He blesses all.
By His knowledge He rules; in His strength He defends;
　　He has love for all.
His birth is our joy; His life is our light; His death has
　　made us conquerors.

St. Mary Magdalen dei Pazzi, born in Florence, Italy, was a Carmelite nun (1566 - 1607). She was one of the spiritual pillars of the Counter-Reformation. Feast: May 25.

COME Holy Spirit. Let the precious pearl of the Father and the Word's delight come.

Spirit of truth, you are the reward of the saints, the comforter of souls, light in the darkness, riches to the poor, treasure to lovers, food for the hungry, comfort to the wanderer; to sum up, You are the one in whom all treasures are contained.

Come! As You descended on Mary, that the Word might become flesh, work in us through grace as You worked in her through nature and grace.

Come! Food of every chaste thought, fountain of all mercy, sum of all purity.

Come! Consume in us whatever prevents us from being consumed in You.

St. Francis de Sales was the Bishop of Geneva, Switzerland (1567 - 1622). He wrote many spiritual books such as *Introduction to the Devout Life* and *The Love of God*. He is the patron of the Catholic Press. Feast: January 24.

SAY not, merciful Virgin, that you cannot help me; for your beloved Son has given you all power in heaven and on earth. Say not that you ought not to assist me, for you are the mother of all the poor children of Adam, and mine in particular.

Since then, merciful Virgin, you are my mother and are all-powerful, what excuse can you offer if you do not lend me your assistance? See, my mother, see, you are obliged to grant me what I ask, and to yield to my entreaties. Amen.

MOST Blessed Virgin, worthy to be made Mother of God, faithful dispenser of the graces which your Son deigns to bestow on us in this life, I beg you, by the love of your divine Son, my Savior, Jesus Christ, to obtain for me of the Holy Spirit, your heavenly Spouse, celestial light and good counsel, by which I may know all I ought to do and how I ought to conform myself for the glory of God and the furtherance of my own salvation.

Most sacred Virgin, I hope to receive this favor of heaven through your intercession; for next to God himself, I place my trust in you. Amen.

O SWEET, Jesus, my Lord, my Savior and my God! Behold me here prostrate before Your majesty, devoting and consecrating this work to Your glory.

Give life to its words by Your blessing, that those souls

for whom I have composed it may receive from it the sacred inspirations that I desire for them.

And in particular, grant them that of imploring for me Your infinite mercy: to the end that while I point out to others the way of devotion in this world, I may not myself be eternally rejected and condemned in the other; but that with them I may forever sing, as a canticle of triumph, the words which with my whole heart I pronounce in testimony of my fidelity amidst the hazards of this mortal life:

LIVE, JESUS! LIVE, JESUS! Yea, Lord Jesus! live and reign in our hearts forever and ever, Amen.

(The preceding is a dedicatory prayer for *Introduction to the Devout Life.*)

Do not fear
  what may happen to you tomorrow.
The same Father
  who cares for you today,
  will care for you tomorrow
  and every other day.
Either He will shield you from suffering
  or He will give you unfailing strength
  to bear it.
Be at peace, then,
  and put aside all
  anxious thoughts
  and imaginings.

St. Aloysius Gonzaga was an Italian Jesuit (1568 - 1591). He died young while nursing the plague-ridden. He has been declared the patron of Catholic youth. Feast: June 21.

O HOLY Mary, my mistress, into your blessed trust and special keeping, into the bosom of your tender mercy, this day, every day of my life and at the hour of my death, I commend my soul and body; to you I entrust all my hopes and consolations, all my trials and miseries, my life and the end of my life, that through your most holy intercession and your merits, all my actions may be ordered and disposed according to your will and that of your divine Son. Amen.

St. Jane Frances de Chantal (1572 - 1641) founded the Order of the Visitation. She was a faithful follower of St. Francis de Sales. Feast: December 12.

O HOLY Mother of the children of God! When shall I rest in your immortal arms? Our souls should be wholly consumed by this desire.

But I will restrain myself and peacefully await the hour which the divine Savior has destined for me, to overwhelm me with that bliss. In the meantime let us have only one desire, to please Him by doing His holy will in all things.

What God wishes for us, let it be done; we are His for time and eternity. Amen.

St. John Brébeuf was a French Jesuit who labored among the Indians of Canada (1593 - 1649). Between 1642 and 1649 he and seven other Jesuits were martyred. His companions were Saints Isaac Jogues, Charles Garnier, Anthony Daniel, Gabriel Lalemant, Noel Chabanel, René Goupil and John de la Lande. Feast: October 19.

JESUS, my Lord and Savior, what can I give You in return for all the favors You have first conferred on me? I will take from Your hand the cup of Your sufferings and call on Your name.

I vow before Your eternal Father and the Holy Spirit, before Your most holy Mother and her most chaste spouse, before the angels, apostles and martyrs, before my blessed fathers St. Ignatius and St. Francis Xavier — in truth, I vow to You, Jesus my Savior, that as far as I have the strength, I will never fail to accept the grace of martyrdom, if someday You in Your infinite mercy should offer it to me, Your most unworthy servant. . . .

My beloved Jesus, here and now I offer my body and blood and life. May I die only for You, if You will grant me this grace, since You willingly died for me. Let me so live that You may grant me the gift of such a happy death. In this way, my God and Savior, I will take from Your hand the cup of Your sufferings and call on Your name: Jesus, Jesus, Jesus!

St. John Berchmans was a Belgian Jesuit scholastic (1599 - 1621). He is the patron saint of acolytes. Feast: August 13.

HOLY Mary, Mother of God and Virgin, I choose you this day for my queen, patron and advocate. I firmly resolve and purpose never to abandon you, never to say or do anything against you, nor to permit anything to be done by others which will dishonor you.

Receive me, then, I beg you, as your perpetual servant; assist me in all my actions and do not abandon me at the hour of my death. Amen.

St. John Eudes was a French priest who founded two congregations of religious (1601 - 1680). He was heroic in his service to the poor. Feast: August 19.

O JESUS my Savior, see me prostrate at Your feet. I adore, I bless and love Your divine providence with all my heart for everything which You will order in the future or permit about my person or about things concerning me; for Your orders and permissions are equally admirable and lovable. Yes, my Savior, Your holy will be done by all and through all, in spite of any repugnance in my heart. Your divine decrees and ordinances shall be blessed and glorified in all eternity.

I realize and confess, O my God, before heaven and earth, that You are just and that I observe these sufferings, and a thousand times more, for the least of my sins. That is the reason why I will embrace this affliction with all my heart to the glory of Your divine justice, in submission to Your sacred will, in honor of the terrible sufferings which You endured on earth, in satisfaction for my sins, in fulfillment of Your plans which You have made about me, and as something that comes from Your most amiable hands and from Your Heart, full of love for me.

Be blessed, O my Jesus, that You have graciously given me an opportunity of suffering for love of You. Let me partake, if it pleases You, of the love, the humility, the patience, the sweetness and the charity with which You suffered; and give me the grace to bear all these sufferings for Your honor and Your pure love. Amen.

HAIL Mary — daughter of God the Father.
Hail Mary — Mother of God the Son.
Hail Mary — Spouse of God the Holy Spirit.
Hail Mary — Temple of the most Blessed Trinity.

Hail Mary — pure lily of the effulgent Trinity.

Hail Mary — celestial rose of the ineffable love of God.

Hail Mary — Virgin pure and humble, of whom the God of heaven willed to be born and with your milk to be nourished.

Hail Mary — Virgin of virgins.

Hail Mary — Queen of martyrs, whose soul was transfixed by a sword.

Hail Mary — Lady most blessed! Unto whom all power in heaven and earth is given.

Hail Mary — my Queen and my mother! my life, my sweetness and my hope.

Hail Mary — Mother most amiable.

Hail Mary — Mother most admirable.

Hail Mary — Mother of divine Love.

Hail Mary — Immaculate; conceived without sin.

Hail Mary full of grace . . .

Blessed be your spouse, St. Joseph.

Blessed be your father, St. Joachim.

Blessed be your mother, St. Anne.

Blessed be your guardian, St. John.

Blessed be the holy angel, St. Gabriel.

Glory be to God the Father who chose you.

Glory be to God the Son who loved you.

Glory be to the Holy Spirit who espoused you.

O Glorious Virgin Mary, may all love and praise you.

Holy Mary, Mother of God, pray for us and bless us, now, and at death in the name of Jesus, your divine Son. Amen.

Blessed Claude de la Colombière was a French Jesuit (1641 - 1682) who was the spiritual director for St. Margaret Mary Alacoque. He was falsely accused in Titus Oates's "popish plot" and exiled from his English mission shortly before his death. Feast: February 15.

O JESUS, You are my true friend, my only friend. You take a part in all my misfortunes; You take them upon Yourself; You know how to change them into blessings.

You listen to me with the greatest kindness when I relate my troubles to You, and You always have balm to pour on my wounds. I find You at all times; I find You everywhere; You never go away; if I have to change my dwelling, I find You wherever I go.

You never weary of listening to me; You are never tired of doing me good. I am certain of being loved by You if I love You; my goods are nothing to You, and by bestowing Yours on me, You never grow poor. However miserable I may be, no one more noble or learned or even holier can come between You and me and deprive me of Your friendship; and death, which tears us away from all other friends, will unite me to You forever.

All the humiliations attached to old age, or to loss of honor, will never detach me from You. On the contrary, I shall never enjoy You more fully, and You will never be closer to me than when everything seems to conspire against me, to overwhelm me and to cast me down.

You bear with all my faults with extreme patience. Even my want of fidelity and my ingratitude do not wound You to such a degree as to make You unwilling to receive me back when I return to You. O Jesus! Grant that I may die praising You, that I may die loving You; that I may die for love of You. Amen.

St. Margaret Mary Alacoque was a French nun (1647 - 1690) who spread devotion to the Sacred Heart of Jesus. She received many private revelations from Christ and, with her confessor, Blessed Claude de la Colombière, she worked to make this devotion a worldwide practice. Feast: October 16.

JESUS Christ, my Lord and my God, whom I believe to be really present in the Blessed Sacrament of the Altar, receive this most profound act of adoration to supply for the desire I have to adore You unceasingly, and in thanksgiving for the sacraments of love which Your Sacred Heart has for me in this sacrament.

I cannot better acknowledge them than by offering You all the acts of adoration, resignation, patience and love which this same Heart has made during its mortal life, and which it makes still and which it shall make eternally in heaven, in order that through it I may love You, praise You, and adore You worthily as much as it is possible for me.

I unite myself to this divine offering which You made to Your Father, and I consecrate to You my whole being, praying You to destroy in me all sin and not to permit that I should be separated from You eternally. Amen.

The Twelve Promises

IN private revelations to St. Margaret Mary, the Sacred Heart made many promises. From her writings these are considered the most important:

1. I will give them all the graces needed for their state in life.
2. I will grant peace in their families.

3. I will console them in all their troubles.

4. I will be their refuge in life and especially in death.

5. I will bless abundantly all their undertakings.

6. Sinners will find in my Heart the source and infinite ocean of mercy.

7. Tepid souls shall become fervent.

8. Fervent souls shall rise speedily to great perfection.

9. I will bless those places where an image of my Sacred Heart is exposed and venerated.

10. I will give to priests the power of touching the most hardened of hearts.

11. Persons who propagate this devotion shall have their names eternally written in my Heart.

12. In the excess of the mercy of my Heart, I promise you that my all-powerful love will grant to all those who will receive Holy Communion on the First Fridays, for nine consecutive months, the grace of final repentance: they will not die in my displeasure, nor without receiving the sacraments; and my Heart will be their secure refuge in that last hour.

O KIND and merciful Savior, from my heart I earnestly desire to return You love for love. My greatest sorrow is that You are not loved by people, and, in particular, that my own heart is so cold, so selfish, so ungrateful.

Keenly aware of my own weakness and poverty, I trust that Your own grace will enable me to offer You an act of pure love. And I wish to offer You this act of love in reparation for the coldness and neglect that are shown to You in the sacrament of Your love by Your creatures.

O Jesus, my supreme good, I love You, not for the sake of the reward which You have promised to those who love You, but purely for Yourself. I love You above all things that can be loved, above all pleasures, and above myself and all that is not You, promising in the presence of heaven and earth that I will live and die purely and simply in Your holy love, and that if to love You thus I must endure persecution and suffering, I am completely satisfied and I will ever say with St. Paul: Nothing will be able to separate us from the love of God.

O Jesus, supreme master of all hearts, I love You, I adore You, I praise You, I thank You, because I am now all Yours. Rule over me and transform my soul into the likeness of Yourself, so that it may bless and glorify You forever in the abode of the saints. Amen.

O HEART of love, I put all my trust in You; for I fear all things from my own weakness, but I hope for all things from Your goodness.

St. Louis-Marie Grignon de Montfort (1673 - 1716) founded the Missionaries of the Company of Mary in the eighteenth century. He is famous for his book *True Devotion to the Blessed Virgin*. Feast: April 28.

HAIL Mary, daughter of God the Father! Hail Mary, mother of God the Son! Hail Mary, spouse of the Holy Spirit! Hail Mary, temple of the most Holy Trinity!

Hail Mary, my mistress, my wealth, my mystic rose, Queen of my heart, my Mother, my life, my sweetness and my dearest hope. I am all yours, and all that I have is yours, O Virgin blessed above all things. May your soul be in me to magnify the Lord; may your spirit be in me to rejoice in God.

Place yourself, O faithful Virgin, as a seal upon my heart, that in you and through you I may be found faithful to God. Grant, most gracious Virgin, that I may be numbered among those whom you are pleased to love, to teach and to guide, to favor and protect as your children.

Grant that with the help of your love I may despise all earthly consolation and cling to heavenly things, until, through the Holy Spirit, your faithful Spouse, and through you, His faithful spouse, Jesus Christ your Son be formed within me for the glory of the Father. Amen.

OUR Father who art in heaven —
    You completely fill heaven and earth
    With the immensity of Your being,
    You are present everywhere;
    You are in the saints by your glory,
    In the damned by Your justice,
    In the good by Your grace,
    Even in sinners, by Your patience, tolerating them.
    Grant that we may always remember that we come

from You and that we may live as Your true children.

Grant that we may set our true course according to Your will and never swerve from You.

Grant that we may use our every power, our hearts and souls and strength to tend toward You, and You alone.

St. Alphonsus Liguori (1696 - 1787) founded the Redemptorists. Within a century of his death he was proclaimed a Doctor of the Church because of his outstanding writings on moral theology. Feast: August 1.

O ST. Teresa, seraphic virgin, beloved spouse of your crucified Lord, who burned with such love for your God and my God while you were on earth, now in paradise you glow with an even brighter love: obtain for me also, I beg you, a spark of that same holy fire which shall cause me to forget this world, all created things, and even myself. You greatly desired to see Him loved by all.

Grant that my every thought and desire and affection may be continually employed in doing the will of God, the supreme Good, whether I am in joy or in pain, for He is worthy to be loved and obeyed everlastingly. Obtain this grace for me, you who are so powerful with God. May I be all on fire, like you, with the holy love of God. Amen.

HOLY Spirit, divine Consoler, I adore You as my true God, with God the Father and God the Son. I adore You and unite myself to the adoration You receive from the angels and saints.

I give You my heart and I offer my ardent thanksgiving for all the grace which You never cease to bestow on me.

O Giver of all supernatural gifts who filled the soul of the Blessed Virgin Mary, Mother of God, with such immense favors, I beg You to visit me with Your grace and Your love and to grant me the gift of holy *fear*, so that it may act on me as a check to prevent me from falling back into my past sins, for which I beg pardon.

Grant me the gift of *piety*, so that I may serve You for the future with increased fervor, follow with more promptness Your holy inspirations, and observe Your divine precepts with greater fidelity.

Grant me the gift of *knowledge*, so that I may know the things of God and, enlightened by Your holy teaching, may walk, without deviation, in the path of eternal salvation.

Grant me the gift of *fortitude*, so that I may overcome courageously all the assaults of the devil, and all the dangers of this world which threaten the salvation of my soul.

Grant me the gift of *counsel*, so that I may choose what is more conducive to my spiritual advancement and may discover the wiles and snares of the tempter.

Grant me the gift of *understanding* so that I may apprehend the divine mysteries and by contemplation of heavenly things detach my thoughts and affections from the vain things of this miserable world.

Grant me the gift of *wisdom* so that I may rightly direct all my actions, referring them to God as my last end; so that, having loved Him and served Him in this life, I may have the happiness of possessing Him eternally in the next. Amen.

O MY God, help me to make a good confession. Mary, my dearest Mother, pray to Jesus for me. Help me to examine my conscience, enable me to obtain true sorrow for my sins, and beg for me the grace rather to die than to offend God again.

Lord Jesus, light of our souls, You enlighten everyone who comes into this world. Enlighten my conscience and my heart by Your Holy Spirit, so that I may perceive all that is displeasing to Your divine majesty and may expiate it by humble confession, true contrition and sincere repentance.

O ADORABLE Infant, I should not dare to present myself before You, except that I know that You invite us. It is I who by my sins caused you to shed so many tears in the stable of Bethlehem, but since You have come to earth to pardon repentant sinners, I ask for Your pardon.

I sincerely repent of having sinned against You who are so good and so full of love for me. The grace that I ask is that I may love You from now on with all my heart. Inflame my soul entirely with Your holy love. I love You, my God who became an Infant for me. Grant that I may never cease to love You.

O Mary, my Mother, you are all-powerful by your prayers. I ask but one favor of You, namely, that You will pray to Jesus for me. Amen.

MOST holy Virgin Immaculate, my Mother Mary, to you who are the Mother of my Lord, the Queen of the universe, the Advocate, the Hope, the Refuge of sinners: I, who am the most miserable of sinners, have recourse to you today.

I venerate you, great queen, and I thank you for the many graces you have obtained for me. I love you, most dear Lady, and because of this love I promise to serve you willingly and to do what I can to make you loved by others.

Since you are so powerful with God, obtain for me the strength to overcome all temptations, until death. Help me have a true love for your Son, Jesus Christ.

Assist me always, but especially at the last moment of my life. Forsake me not then until you see me safely in heaven. Such is my hope. Amen.

MY Jesus, I believe that You are present in the Blessed Sacrament. I love You above all things and I desire You in my soul. Since I cannot now receive You sacramentally, come at least spiritually into my heart. As though You were already there, I embrace You and unite myself wholly to You. Do not permit that I should ever be separated from You.

JESUS Christ my God, I adore You and I thank You for all the graces You have given me today. I offer You my sleep and all the moments of this night and I beg You to keep me without sin.

I place myself within Your Sacred Heart and under the mantle of our Lady, my Mother. Let Your holy angels stand beside me and keep me in peace. Let your blessing be on me.

THE Way of the Cross (Stations) was an ancient devotion brought from the Holy Land, where pilgrims traced the footsteps of Christ, especially on the *Via Dolorosa,* the road to Calvary. This devotion has been promoted for several centuries through the prayers of St. Alphonsus.

FIRST STATION: *Jesus Is Condemned to Death*

Consider how Jesus, after having been scourged and crowned with thorns, was unjustly condemned by Pilate to die on the cross.

My adorable Jesus, it was not Pilate, no, it was my sins that condemned You to death. I beg You, by the merits of this sorrowful journey, to assist my soul in its journey toward eternity.

I love You, Jesus my love, I love You more than myself; I repent with my whole heart for having offended You. Never permit me to separate myself from You again. Grant that I may love You always and then do with me as You will.

SECOND STATION: *Jesus Takes Up His Cross*

Consider how Jesus, in making this journey with the cross on His shoulders, thought of us, and for us offered to His Father the death He was about to undergo.

My beloved Jesus, I embrace all the tribulations You have destined for me until death. I beg You, by the merits of the pain You suffered for me in carrying Your cross, to give me the necessary help to carry mine with perfect patience and resignation.

I love You, Jesus my love . . .

THIRD STATION: *Jesus Falls the First Time*

Consider this first fall of Jesus under His cross. His flesh was torn with scourges, His head crowned with thorns, and He had lost a great quantity of blood. He was so weakened He could scarcely walk, and yet He had to carry this great load upon His shoulders. The soldiers struck Him rudely, and thus He fell several times in His journey.

My beloved Jesus, it is not the weight of the cross, but my sins, which have made You suffer so much pain. Ah, by the merits of this first fall, deliver me from the misfortune of falling into mortal sin.

I love You, Jesus my love . . .

FOURTH STATION: *Jesus Meets His Afflicted Mother*

Consider the meeting of the Son and the Mother, which took place on this journey. Jesus and Mary looked at each other, and their looks became as so many arrows to wound those hearts which loved each other so tenderly.

My most loving Jesus, by the sorrow You experienced in this meeting, grant me the grace of a truly devoted love for Your most holy Mother. And you, my Queen, overwhelmed with sorrow, obtain for me, by your intercession, a continual and tender remembrance of the Passion of your Son.

I love You, Jesus my love . . .

FIFTH STATION: *Simon of Cyrene Helps Jesus*

Consider how the Jews, seeing that at each step Jesus from weakness was on the point of expiring, and fearing that He would die on the way, when they wished Him to die the ignominious death of the cross, constrained Simon the Cyrenian to carry the cross behind Our Lord.

My most sweet Jesus, I will not refuse the cross as the Cyrenian did; I accept it, I embrace it. I accept in particular the death You have destined for me; with all the pains that may accompany it; I unite it to Your death, I offer it to You. You have died for love of me; I will die for love of You and to please You. Help me by Your grace.

I love You, Jesus my love . . .

SIXTH STATION: *Veronica Wipes the Face of Jesus*

Consider how the holy woman named Veronica, seeing Jesus so afflicted, and His face bathed in sweat and blood, presented Him with a towel with which He wiped His adorable face, leaving on it the impression of His holy countenance.

My most beloved Jesus, Your face was beautiful before, but in this journey it has lost all its beauty, and wounds and blood have disfigured it. Alas, my soul was once beautiful, when it received Your grace in Baptism; but I have disfigured it since by my sins; You alone, my Redeemer, can restore it to its former beauty. Do this by Your passion; O Jesus. I repent of having offended You. Never permit me to offend You again.

I love You, Jesus my love . . .

SEVENTH STATION: *Jesus Falls the Second Time*

Consider the second fall of Jesus under the cross — a fall which renews that pain of all the wounds of the head and members of our afflicted Lord.

My most gentle Jesus, how many times You have pardoned me, and how many times I have fallen again, and begun again to offend You! Oh, by the merits of this new fall, give me the necessary help to persevere in Your grace until death. Grant that in all temptations which assail me, I may always commend myself to You.
I love You, Jesus my love . . .

EIGHTH STATION: *Jesus Comforts the Women of Jerusalem*

Consider how these women wept with compassion at seeing Jesus in such a pitiable state, streaming with blood, as He walked along. But Jesus said to them, "Weep not for me but for yourselves and for your children."

My Jesus, laden with sorrows, I weep for the offenses I have committed against You, because of the pains they have deserved, and still more because of the displeasure they have caused You who have loved me so much. It is Your love, more than the fear of hell which causes me to weep for my sins.
I love You, Jesus my love . . .

NINTH STATION: *Jesus Falls the Third Time*

Consider the third fall of Jesus Christ. His weakness was extreme, and the cruelty of his executioners excessive, who tried to hasten His steps when He had scarcely strength to move.

Ah, my outraged Jesus, by the merits of the weakness You suffered in going up Calvary, give me strength sufficient to conquer all human respect and all my wicked passions which have led me to despise Your friendship.
I love You, Jesus my love . . .

TENTH STATION: *Jesus Is Stripped of His Garments*

Consider the violence with which the executioners stripped Jesus. His inner garments adhered to His torn flesh, and they dragged them off so roughly that the skin came with them. Compassionate your Savior thus cruelly treated and say to Him:

My innocent Jesus, by the merits of the torment You felt, help me to strip myself of all affection to things of earth, in order that I may place all my love in You who are so worthy of my love.

I love You, Jesus my love . . .

ELEVENTH STATION: *Jesus is Nailed to the Cross*

Consider how Jesus, after being thrown on the cross, extended His hands and offered to His eternal Father the sacrifice of His death for our salvation. These barbarians fastened Him with nails, and then, raising the cross, allowed Him to die with anguish on this infamous gibbet.

My Jesus! loaded with contempt, nail my heart to Your feet, that it may ever remain there, to love You and never quit You again.

I love You, Jesus my love . . .

TWELFTH STATION: *Jesus Dies on the Cross*

Consider how your Jesus, after three hours' agony on the cross, consumed at length with anguish, abandons himself to the weight of His body, bows His head and dies.

O my dying Jesus, I kiss devoutly the cross on which You died for love of me. I have merited by my sins to die a miserable death, but Your death is my hope. Ah, by the merits of Your death, give me grace to die embracing Your feet and burning with love for You. I yield my soul into Your hands.

I love You, Jesus my love. . .

THIRTEENTH STATION: *Jesus Is Taken Down*
     from the Cross

Consider how, after the death of Our Lord, two of His disciples, Joseph and Nicodemus, took Him down from the cross, and placed Him in the arms of His afflicted Mother, who received Him with unutterable tenderness, and pressed Him to her bosom.

O Mother of Sorrow, for the love of this Son, accept me as your servant and pray to Him for me. And You, my holy Redeemer, since You have died for me, permit me to love You, for I wish but You and nothing more.

I love You, Jesus my love . . .

FOURTEENTH STATION: *Jesus Is Laid in the Tomb*

Consider how the disciples carried the body of Jesus to bury it, accompanied by His Holy Mother, who arranged it in the sepulcher with her own hands. They then closed the tomb and all withdrew.

O my buried Jesus, I kiss the stone that encloses You. But You rose to life again on the third day. I beg You, by Your Resurrection, make me rise glorious with You at the last day, to be always united with You in heaven, to praise and love You forever.

I love You, Jesus my love . . .

(Some modern Stations include a fifteenth station on the Resurrection.)

V

Toward the Modern Church

THAT phrase "modern Church" is quite subjective. For us it means the Church of the post-Vatican II era. The saints are still out there, working for and in the Church, but someone else will have to add that section.

The events in the world really overshadowed the interior growth of the Church during the Industrial Revolution, the American Revolution and the French Revolution. Modernism, the Masons, Jansenism and anticlericalism conspired against Christianity.

Yet, the saints were there, from St. John Vianney to St. Thérèse of Lisieux and the spiritual giant St. John Bosco. Saints from North and South America were finally being recognized, but we have little of their writings and few of their prayers. Saints from the Third World will also soon take their places in compilations such as this, but, again, that's for a future editor.

For now, this section must end with St. Frances Cabrini, the first canonized American citizen, and St. Maximilian Kolbe, that noble example of a priest.

It's a worthy conclusion.

Blessed Crescentia Hoess was a Franciscan nun who was noted for her devotion to the ideals of poverty of spirit (1682 - 1744). She reached mystical heights in prayer. Feast: April 5.

GRANT, O God, that love and suffering may grow hand in hand in me,
So that I may love You more and more
With the cheerful disposition which is the fruit of love.
O Lord, only grant me love for You, and I shall be rich enough.
I desire only that You leave me to my nothingness and that You alone, if I may say so, be all in all and loved and honored by everybody.
I wish to take pleasure in nothing but only in You and Your love.

St. Paul of the Cross was an Italian religious (1694 - 1775) who founded the Passionists. His religious take a special vow to promote devotion to the Passion of Christ. Feast: October 19.

LORD, I give thanks to You for Your dying on the Cross for my sins.

St. Benedict Joseph Labre was called "the beggar of Rome" (1748 - 1783). He was known for his devotion to the Forty Hours. Feast: April 16.

JESUS Christ, King of Glory, came in peace. God was made man. The Word was made flesh. Christ was born of the Virgin Mary. Christ walked in peace through the midst of them. Christ was crucified. Christ died. Christ was buried. Christ rose again. Christ ascended into heaven. Christ conquers. Christ reigns. Christ commands. May Christ defend us from all evil. Jesus is with us.

St. Clement Mary Hofbauer (1751 - 1820) was the Re-demptorist who brought his congregation beyond its Italian beginnings. He was subjected to many dangers from anticlericals. Feast: March 15.

O MY Redeemer, will that terrible moment ever come when but few Christians shall be left who are in-spired by the spirit of faith, that moment when Your in-dignation shall be provoked and Your protection shall be taken from us?

Have our vices and our evil lives irrevocably moved Your justice to take vengeance, perhaps this very day, upon Your children? We beg You, the Beginning and the End of Faith, with contrite hearts, not to let the light of faith be extinguished in souls.

Remember Your mercies of old, turn Your eyes in compassion upon the vineyard planted by Your own right hand, and watered by the tears of the Apostles, by the pre-cious blood of countless martyrs, and made fruitful by the prayers of so many confessors and innocent virgins.

O divine Mediator, look upon those zealous souls who raise their hearts to You and pray without ceasing for the maintenance of that most precious gift of Yours, the True Faith. Keep us safe in the true Catholic and Roman Faith. Preserve us in Your holy faith, for if we are rich with this precious gift, we shall gladly endure every sorrow and nothing shall ever be able to change our happiness.

On the other hand, without this great treasure of the faith, our unhappiness would be unspeakable and without limit. O Good Jesus, Author of our faith, preserve it pure within us; keep us safe in the bark of Peter, faithful and obedient to his successor and Your vicar here on earth, so that the unity of the holy Church may be maintained, holi-ness fostered, the Holy See protected in freedom, and the Church universal extended to the benefit of souls.

O Jesus, Author of our faith, humble and convert the enemies of Your Church; grant true peace and concord to all Christian kings and princes and to all believers; strengthen and preserve us in Your holy service, to the end that we may live with You and die in You.

O Jesus, Author of our faith, let me live for You and die for You. Amen.

St. Madeleine Sophie Barat (1779 - 1865) founded the Religious of the Sacred Heart. In 1818 she sent Mother Rose Philippine Duchesne to found schools in the United States. Feast: May 25.

WHEN the love of Jesus is in question, let our generosity know no bounds; we can never bear enough for the God Who suffered so much for us.

Let us love the Heart of Jesus the more, since it is wonderful and forgotten by so many. And if we, favored as we are, give Him but half a heart, what do we deserve?

Love God, and if you cannot meditate always say, "My God I love You."

How blind we are! When all earthly love passes away, we entrust ourselves to the loyal love of You, Lord Jesus, our Friend. Amen.

St. John Vianney (1786 - 1859) is the famous French diocesan priest known popularly as the "Curé of Ars." He was devoted to working with the Sacrament of Reconciliation. Feast: August 4.

O MOST Holy Virgin Mary, you stand ever before the most Holy Trinity and continually intercede for us with your most beloved Son; pray for me in all my necessities; help me, combat for me and obtain for me the pardon of all my sins. Help me especially in my last hour; and when I can no longer give any sign of the use of reason, encourage me, make the sign of the cross for me, and fight for me against the enemy.

Make a profession of faith in my name; favor me with a testimony of my salvation and never let me despair of the mercy of God. Help me to overthrow the wicked enemy. When I can no longer say, "Jesus, Mary and Joseph, I place my soul in your hands," please say it for me; when I can no longer hear human words of consolation, comfort me.

Leave me not before I have been judged; and if I have to expiate for my sins in purgatory, O! pray for me earnestly; and admonish my friends to procure for me a speedy enjoyment of the blessed sight of God. Lessen my suffering, deliver me speedily and lead my soul into heaven with you: that, united with all the elect, I may there bless and praise my God and you for all eternity. Amen.

MY Jesus, from all eternity You planned to give Yourself to us in this sacrament of Your love. Therefore, You planted within us such a longing that it may only be satisfied by Yourself.

I may go from here to the other end of the world, from one country to another, from riches to greater riches, from pleasure to pleasure, and still I shall not be content. All the world cannot satisfy the immortal soul. It would be like trying to satisfy a starving person with a grain of corn.

It is good when we set our hearts, our imperfect hearts, on loving You, my God. We were made for charity: that is why we are so prone to love. But we are such that nothing in this world can satisfy us. Only when we turn to God can we be contented.

It happens sometimes that the more we know our neighbor, the less we love him, but with You, O God, it is never so. The more we know You the more we love You. Knowledge of You kindles such a fire of love in our souls that no room is left for other love and longing.

My Jesus, how good it is to love You! Let me be like Your disciples on Mt. Tabor, seeing nothing else but You, my Savior. Let us be as two friends, neither of whom can ever bear to offend the other. Amen.

Blessed Vincent Pallotti (1795 - 1850) organized Catholic Action almost a century before it became popular in Europe. He was an important spiritual guide for the laity of his time. Feast: January 22.

IMMACULATE Mother of God, Queen of heaven, Mother of mercy, Advocate and Refuge of sinners! Enlightened and inspired by the grace obtained for me so richly from the divine treasury through your maternal affection, I resolve this day and always to place my heart in your hands to be consecrated to Jesus.

To you, therefore, most Blessed Virgin, I now give it, in the presence of the nine choirs of angels and all the saints. In my name, consecrate it to Jesus. Because of the childlike confidence which I have in you, I am certain that now and always you will do all you can to make my heart belong entirely to Jesus, so that I may imitate perfectly the example of the saints, and in particular Saint Joseph, your most pure spouse. Amen.

St. John Bosco (1818 - 1888) was an Italian priest who founded the Salesians. He co-founded the Daughters of Mary, Help of Christians. Feast: January 31.

O MARY, powerful Virgin, you are the mighty and glorious protector of the Church; you are the marvelous help of Christians; you are terrible as an army set in battle array; you alone have destroyed every heresy in the whole world.

In the midst of our anguish, our struggles and our distress, defend us from the power of the enemy and at the hour of our death receive our souls in paradise. Amen.

St. Gabriel of the Sorrowful Mother (1838 - 1862) was an Italian Passionist. He died while he was still a scholastic. Feast: February 27.

BEHOLD me at Your feet, O Lord, begging for pity and mercy. What will You lose in granting me a great love for You, deep humility, great purity of heart and mind and body, fraternal charity, intense sorrow for having offended You, and the grace to offend You no more?

What will You lose, O my God, by enabling me to receive worthily Your Son in Holy Communion, by assisting me to act through love of You in all my thoughts, works, penances and prayers, by granting me the grace of loving Your holy mother most tenderly and trustfully, the grace of persevering and of dying a good and holy death?

I am Your beggar, covered with sores and rags, asking for alms; Oh, look upon my misery! Behold my proud head, my cold and stony heart; behold my mind filled with worldly thoughts, my will inclined only to evil, my body rebellious to every good work.

Help me, O my God; help me to conquer myself! This I ask through Your infinite mercy. To obtain it, I offer You the merits of Jesus Christ, our Savior and Lord. I have no merits of my own; I am destitute, but His wounds will be my plea. Had I shed my blood for love of You, like Your Son, would you grant me this favor? How much more should You hear me, since He shed His Blood for me?

You promised in Your Gospel that whatever I request for the good of my soul, You would grant: "Ask and you shall receive." Now, since You cannot withdraw Your word, I beg You through Your infinite goodness, through the Heart of Your Son wounded with love for me, through the infinite charity of Your most holy daughter, Mary, and for the honor of the whole heavenly court, into which I ask You one day to admit me. Amen.

St. Gemma Galgani lived in Italy at the turn of the past century (1878 - 1903). Her short life was filled with many extraordinary happenings. Feast: April 11.

O MY crucified God, behold me at Your feet; do not cast me out, now that I appear before You as a sinner. I have offended You exceedingly in the past, my Jesus, but it shall be so no longer.

Before You, O Lord, I place all my sins; I have now considered Your own sufferings and see how great is the worth of that Precious Blood that flows from Your veins.

O my God, at this hour close Your eyes to my want of merit, and since You have been pleased to die for my sins, grant me forgiveness for them all, that I may no longer feel the burden of my sins, for this burden, Dear Jesus, oppresses me beyond measure.

Assist me, my Jesus, for I desire to become good whatsoever it may cost; take away, destroy, utterly root out all that You find in me contrary to Your holy will. At the same time, I pray You, Lord Jesus, to enlighten me that I may be able to walk in Your holy light. Amen.

Pope St. Pius X (1835 - 1914) had extensive pastoral experience before being elevated to the papacy. The most glorious actions were his decrees urging the frequent reception of Holy Communion and lowering the age for First Holy Communion. Feast: August 21.

O MOST sweet Jesus, who came into this world to give to all souls the life of Your grace, and who, to preserve and increase it in them, willed to be the daily Remedy of their weakness and the Food for each day, we humbly beseech You, by Your Heart so burning with love for us, to pour Your divine Spirit upon all souls in order that those who have the misfortune to be in the state of mortal sin may, returning to You, find the life of grace which they have lost.

Through this same Holy Spirit, may those who are already living by this divine life devoutly approach Your divine Table every day when it is possible, so that, receiving each day in Holy Communion the antidote of their daily venial sins and each day sustaining in themselves the life of Your grace and thus ever purifying themselves the more, they may finally come to a happy life with You. Amen.

St. Thérèse of Lisieux (1873 - 1897) was a French Carmelite who became a nun at the age of fifteen. Her "little way of spiritual perfection" is still very popular. Feast:
October 1.

O JESUS, who in Your cruel passion became the "Re-
proach of men and the Man of Sorrows," I worship Your
divine face. Once it shone with the beauty and sweetness
of the Divinity; now for my sake it has become the face of
a leper.

Yet in that disfigured countenance I recognize Your infinite love and I am consumed with the desire for loving
You and of making You loved by all mankind. The tears
that streamed in such abundance from Your eyes are to
me as precious pearls which I delight to gather, that with
their infinite worth I may ransom the souls of poor sinners.

O Jesus, whose face is the sole beauty that ravishes
my heart, I may not behold here upon earth the sweetness
of Your glance, nor feel the ineffable tenderness of Your
kiss. I consent to this, but I pray You to imprint in me
Your divine likeness, and I implore You so to inflame me
with Your love that it may quickly consume me, and soon I
may reach the vision of Your glorious face in heaven!
Amen.

I HAVE realized that whoever undertakes to do anything for the sake of earthly things or to earn the praise of
others, deceives himself.

Today one thing pleases the world, tomorrow another;
and what is praised on one occasion is denounced on another.

Blessed be You, my Lord and my God, for You are un-
changeable for all eternity. Whoever serves You faithfully
to the end will enjoy life without end in eternity. Amen.

Abandonment to God

I CONSIDER that "all is vanity but to love God and serve Him alone."

The grace which I especially ask, O Jesus, is never to offend You.

My gifts are all unworthy, and so I offer You my very soul, O most loving Savior.

I fear only one thing, my God, to keep my own will. Take it, therefore, for I choose all that You choose.

It is confidence and nothing else that leads one to Love. And what offends Jesus, what wounds His Heart, is lack of trust in Him.

If souls, who are as feeble and as imperfect as I, could feel as I feel, no one would despair of reaching the summit of the mountain of love. Jesus, indeed, does not demand great deeds, but only self-surrender and gratitude.

O my Beloved, I offer myself to You, that You may perfectly accomplish in me Your holy designs, and I will not allow anything created to be an obstacle to their accomplishment.

St. Francis Xavier Cabrini (1850 - 1917) was the first American citizen ever canonized. Her work among Italian immigrants took her to many nations around the world. Feast: November 13.

FORTIFY me with the grace of Your Holy Spirit and give Your peace to my soul that I may be free from all needless anxiety, solicitude and worry. Help me to desire always that which is pleasing and acceptable to You so that Your will may be my will.

Grant that I may rid myself of all unholy desires and that, for Your love, I may remain obscure and unknown in this world, to be known only to You. Do not permit me to attribute to myself the good that You perform in me and through me, but rather, referring all honor to Your Majesty, may I glory only in my infirmities, so that renouncing sincerely all vainglory which comes from the world, I may aspire to that true and lasting glory which comes from You. Amen.

St. Maximilian Kolbe (1894 - 1941), was a Polish conventual Franciscan martyred under the Nazis at Auschwitz. He was devoted to the Blessed Sacrament, the Blessed Mother and the medium of the press. Feast: August 14.

LOVE the Immaculata, love the Immaculata, love the Immaculata!

Confide in her. Consecrate yourself to her entirely and without reserve. I wish you to love her so much as to be incapable of living without her.

Try to do everything as she herself would do it in your place, especially by loving God as she loves Him. Amen.

(The Saint adds, "You can only learn this on your knees.")

LET me praise you, O most holy Virgin!

Let me praise you at my own cost.

Let me live, work, waste away and die for you alone.

Let me contribute to your exaltation, to your highest exaltation.

Permit that others may outdo my zeal in glorifying you, O Mary, so that by holy rivalry your glory may grow more rapidly, just as He wills it, who raised you above all creatures.

In you alone, God has been more adored than in all other saints,

For you God created the world, and for you He created me also.

O let me praise you, most holy Virgin Mary.

VI

Appendix: Other Favorite Prayers

IN researching for a volume like this, I came across so many beautiful prayers that I couldn't use because of the stated nature of this work.

I couldn't help adding a few of my favorites as an appendix. They show that the Holy Spirit is at work in the Church in all the walks of life, in the canonized saints and in special people God raises up in various times and places.

I have used these prayers for years; I'm sure you could add to the list.

Mary Stuart, more familiarly known as Mary Queen of Scots (1542 - 1587), was beheaded at the bidding of Queen Elizabeth I of England.

KEEP me, O God, from pettiness.
Let us be large in thought, word and deed.
Let us be done with fault-finding and leave off self-seeking. May we put away all pretense and meet each other face to face without self-pity and without prejudice.
May we never be hasty in judgment and always generous.
Let us take time for all things.
Make us grow calm, serene, gentle.
Teach us to put into action our better impulses, and make us straightforward and unafraid.
Grant that we may realize that it is the little things in life that create differences; that in the big things we are all one.
And, O Lord God,
Let us not forget to be kind.

Fray Junipero Serra was known as the "apostle" of California (1713 - 1784). He founded nine of the twenty-one Franciscan missions in what is now the state of California.

HAPPY are they who have a son as a priest, who every day, in the Holy Sacrifice of the Mass, prays for them as best he can, and very often offers for them exclusively his Mass, so that the Lord sends them help:

That they have the necessities of life; that God may grant them the grace of patience in their trials, of resignation to His holy will, peace and union with their neighbors, courage to resist the temptations of the devil, and finally, at the proper time, a happy death in His holy grace. Amen.

Cardinal John Henry Newman (1801 - 1890) contributed greatly to the life of the Catholic Church in England during the nineteenth century. His conversion to Rome was noted in the newspapers of his day and in the Parliament. The Friends of Cardinal Newman are working for his canonization.

MAY the Lord support us all the day long.
Till the shades lengthen and the evening comes,
And the busy world is hushed
   and the fever of life is over,
And our work is done.

Then in His mercy may He give us
   A safe lodging,
   A holy rest,
And peace at the last. Amen.

Lead, Kindly Light

LEAD, kindly light, amid th' encircling gloom,
   Lead Thou me on!
The night is dark and I am far from home,
   Lead Thou me on, lead Thou me on!

Keep Thou my feet, I do not ask to see
   The distant scene;
One step enough for me, one step enough for me.

I was not ever thus, nor prayed, that Thou shouldst
   Lead me on;
I loved to choose and see my path, but now, but now
   Lead Thou me on.

I loved the garish day and 'spite of fears,
Pride ruled my will, pride ruled my will
Remember not past years, remember not past years,
So long Thy power has blessed me.

Sure it still will lead me on,
O'er moor and fen, o'er crag and torrent, till
The night, the night is gone, and with the morn
   Those angel faces smile,

Which I have loved long since, and lost awhile.
And with the morn, those angel faces smile,
Which I have loved long since,
   And lost a while.

                              (Hymn version)

Abbot Columba Marmion (1858 - 1923) was the venerable Benedictine abbot of Maredsou in Belgium. He was the great pioneer of the liturgical movement which culminated in the work of Vatican II.

How good it is to repeat, now, the prayer of Jesus himself, the beloved Son of the Father, which, placed on our lips through Him, is pre-eminently the prayer of the child of God: O holy Father, You who dwell in Heaven, we are Your children since You willed to have us call You "Father."

May Your Name be honored, loved and glorified! May Your perfections be praised and exalted more and more on the earth. May we manifest in ourselves, by our works, the splendor of Your grace.

Extend Your reign; may Your Kingdom ever increase, this Kingdom which is also that of Your Son, since You have made Him its Head. May Your Son be truly the King of our souls, and may we testify to his reign over us by the perfect accomplishment of Your will.

May we, like Him, ever seek to adhere to You by fulfilling Your good pleasure (John 8:29), Your eternal designs for us, so as to be like to Jesus in all things, and through Him, worthy children of Your love. Amen.

(Christ, the Life of the Soul)

Let us adore this holy, immaculate High Priest, who is God's own Son; let us cast ourselves down before this Mediator who alone, because He is at once God and Man, can fully realize His mission of salvation and render to us

God's gifts by the sacrifice of His humanity; but let us likewise confide ourselves to His divine virtue which, also alone, was powerful enough to reconcile us with the Father. Amen.

(Christ in His Mysteries)

Cardinal Rafael Merry del Val (1865 - 1930) was the Secretary of State for Pope St. Pius X. Despite all the pomp and circumstance of his position, he led a spiritual life built on charity and humility.

Litany of Humility

O JESUS, meek and humble of heart, hear me.

From the desire of being esteemed, *deliver me Lord Jesus.*

From the desire of being extolled, *deliver me . . .*

From the desire of being honored,

From the desire of being praised,

From the desire of being preferred before others,

From the desire of being consulted,

From the desire of being approved,

From the desire of being highly regarded,

From the fear of being humiliated,

From the fear of being rebuked,

From the fear of being forgotten,

From the fear of being wronged,

From the fear of being suspected,

That others may be loved more than I, *Jesus grant me the grace to desire it.*

That in the opinion of the world, others may increase and I decrease . . .

That others may be chosen and I passed over . . .

That others be praised and I go unnoticed . . .

That others should be preferred before me in everything. . .

That others may become holier than I, provided that I may become as holy as I should . . . .

Bishop Charles Francis Buddy (1887 - 1966) founded
the Diocese of San Diego, California, in 1936. For almost
thirty years he led the Church there and wrote books on
apologetics, homilies and a famous prayer book.

HOLY Spirit of Wisdom and of love, we ask
You, through the intercession of Our Lady of Good Counsel, to direct the deliberations of our meeting today.

O divine Comforter, send forth Your Spirit to enlighten
our minds, fortify our wills and inflame our hearts with
divine Love. Intensify our resolve to use the powerful influence of unified strength under the standard of the Cross
to help one another.

O heavenly Father, extend the scope of our usefulness,
that by loyal cooperation with holy Mother Church our
apostolate of Catholic action may attract and lead souls to
heaven through the merits of Our Lord Jesus Christ.
Amen.

The Authors: Alphabetical Index

Name	Dates	Feast	Pg.
St. Mary Magdalen dei Pazzi	1566 - 1607	May 25	*139*
St. Matthew, Apostle	1st cent.	Sept. 21	*12*
St. Maximilian Kolbe	1894 - 1941	Aug. 14	*180*
St. Nicetas	335 - 415	Jun. 22	*53*
St. Odo of Cluny	879 - 942	Nov. 18	*72*
St. Paschal Baylon	1540 - 1592	May 17	*132*
St. Patrick	389 - 461	Mar. 17	*54*
St. Paul, Apostle	1st cent.	Jun. 29	*20*
St. Paul of the Cross	1694 - 1775	Oct. 19	*165*
St. Paulinus	726 - 802	Jan. 28	*69*
St. Peter, Apostle	1st cent.	Jun. 29	*23*
St. Peter Canisius	1521 - 1597	Dec. 21	*130*
St. Peter Damian	1007 - 1072	Feb. 21	*74*
St. Pius V, Pope	1504 - 1572	Apr. 30	*125*
St. Pius X, Pope	1835 - 1914	Aug. 21	*176*
St. Polycarp	2nd cent.	Feb. 23	*29*
St. Richard of Chichester	1197 - 1253	Apr. 3	*86*
St. Robert Bellarmine	1542 - 1621	Sept. 17	*134*
St. Robert Southwell	1561 - 1595	Feb. 21	*138*
St. Simon Stock	Died 1265	May 16	*107*
St. Teresa of Avila	1515 - 1582	Oct. 15	*128*
St. Thérèse of Lisieux	1873 - 1897	Oct. 1	*177*
St. Thomas Aquinas	1225 - 1274	Jan. 28	*91*
St. Thomas More	1478 - 135	Jun. 22	*121*
St. Venantius Fortunatus	530 - 609	Dec. 14	*60*
St. Vincent Ferrer	1350 - 1418	Apr. 5	*113*
Bd. Vincent Pallotti	1795 - 1850	Jan. 22	*172*

Appendix:

Name	Dates	Pg.
Buddy, Bishop Charles Francis	1542 - 1587	*189*
Marmion, Abbot Columba	1848 - 1923	*186*
Merry del Val, Cardinal Rafael	1865 - 1930	*188*
Newman, Cardinal John Henry	1801 - 1890	*184*
Serra, Fray Junipero	1713 - 1784	*183*
Stuart, Mary, Queen of Scots	1542 - 1587	*182*

General Subject Index

Additional prayer books from OSV

Everyday Prayers for Everyday People
by Bernadette McCarver Snyder
No. 604, paper, $4.95

Prayer Book of the Bible:
Reflections on the Old Testament
by Rev. Peter M.J. Stravinskas
No. 606, paper, $5.95

A World at Prayer
by Rev. Robert J. Fox
No. 633, paper, $3.95

A Prayer Book for Young Catholics
by Rev. Robert J. Fox
No. 637, leatherette, $4.95

A Catholic Prayer Book
by Rev. Robert J. Fox
No. 771, paper, $3.95

A Book of Prayers
No. 667, leatherette, $4.95